# Freezer Meals

## *Make-Ahead Slow Cooker Recipes*

©*Jade Blake*

# Forward

I would like to thank you for purchasing "Freezer Meals: Make-Ahead Slow Cooker Recipes" and congratulate you for taking important steps to improve your health and wellbeing.

Slow cooker freezer meals are a real game-changer. Whether you've made slow cooker freezer meals before or are brand-new to freezer cooking this book will share all the things that you need to know to make all of your freezer meals a massive success.

Are you ready to save your valuable time and money?

Freezer Meals reboot your system to get rid of all the negative eating habits such as sugar addiction and gives you another shot at finding balance in your life, as you now prepare your food consciously well before the time which eliminates the tendency to use sub-par ingredients and cheat by eating fast-foods.

Mealtimes have never been more streamlined.

This book will use a step-wise approach to take you through the Freezer Meal Slow Cooker Planand further beyond into the practical application of making healthy and super tasty recipes. Freezer Meals expounds on a practical and sustainable way to nourish our bodies to maintain lifelong health, physical performance and overall wellness- all while letting you spend time on the things that matter most-friends, family and hobbies.

We are going to look at organic, hearty, healthy slow cooker recipes bursting with flavors that are 100 percent natural and organic that will rev up your metabolism and satisfy your appetite with every bite.

These can be cooked straight from the freezer and require no extra preparation once sealed in their bag.

Wait a second… did we mention weight loss?

Embrace the Freezer Meals diet and you will fit into your favorite pair of jeans in no time!

# Table of Contents

# Frozen In Time

*"Now I saw this categorizing of my freezer food as a sign of the true chaos in my head."*

*- Abraham Verghese*

Life is busy. Every single one of us gets caught up in our own personal projects, hobbies, sports, movies books and games- and who wouldn't want to? These are the things of leisure that we love to spend time on. The problem arises when we've been completely absorbed in something and then suddenly we take a look at the clock, shocked: *It's dinner time already?!?*

What happens on nights like these – when you haven't planned, and you're too tired to fix a nutritious meal? The take-out line or drive-through beckons. This option is not only bad for you're budget, but even worse for your waistline.

It's a sad thought that in today's fast paced society, fast food and processed packaged meals have taken the place of a good home cooked dinner

Is there not a way to get the best of both worlds? You're in luck.

With the help of one of the most underused appliances in most people's kitchen -- the freezer - absolutely ANYONE can create and store two weeks' worth of delicious home-cooked meals in a matter of just a few hours.

## Is the Food Still As Nutritious Once Frozen?

To put it simply: Yes.

Well prepared frozen food loses its nutrients very, very slowly over time. Freezing is the BEST option to preserve food.

Another important contributing factor is the method of cooking used before freezing. Baking, blanching and steaming are all healthy ways of preparing food that lend well to freezing. A great option is to prepare all the ingredients in sealable bags, uncooked, with the sauce in a separate bag, so that all you have to do is defrost, cook, and enjoy.

## What Will I Need?

If you're eager to get started here is what you'll need:

- Appliance for cooking and reheating- Stove top, microwave and/or oven.
- Sealable freezer storage bags(Ziplocs) and containers in various sizes.
- A few different coloured permanent marker for labelling OR printable labels(both work just fine)
- Freezer space: consider how much you are able to store at a time to meet you day to day requirements
- Optional: crock pot- make life a lot easier ; food processor/blender

There are a various ways to do freezer cooking. Some prefer to have one big cooking day per month. Others will make double batches of all their meals to store in the freezer for later. Choose whatever works best for you and your family

## What I Can Freeze?

Lasagne's, soups, stews and casseroles are the usual suspects when it comes to freezing. The meals and sides that people often forget are things like like pasta sauces, meatballs, seasoned and marinated meats, poultry, burritos and vegetable fillings for tacos. Mini "meal- kits are another viable option, consisting of sliced meat and vegetables prepped for cooking later for fajitas and stir-fries. Add some Ziploc bags of tortillas, beans, and already cooked rice and you're on your way.

Here are a few ingredients that freeze very well:

- Butter can be frozen for 3 months.
- Cheese can be frozen for up to 4 months and can be used straight from the freezer.
- Most bread will freeze well for up to 3 months. Sliced bread can be toasted from frozen.
- Milk will freeze for 1 month. Defrost in the fridge and shake well before using.
- Raw pastry will freeze for for 6 months and will take about 1 hour to thaw completely.

Even foods that don't seem freezer friendly can be tweaked slightly. Do some of the prep if you can't do it all in advance.

# Pro Tips for Freezing

**1. Always Cool foods** before you freeze them. Trying to freeze food when hot will increase the temperature of the freezer causing other foods valuable foodstuffs to start defrosting.

**2. Re-freezing** anything that's been frozen is a big NO. Even if the food was frozen raw and then cooked, to be extra safe it still shouldn't be re-frozen.

**3. Save money with a full freezer:** Cold air doesn't need to circulate as much, so less power is needed making it a lot more economical to have a full freezer. If you have lots of space free, be sure to fill plastic bottles half full with water and use them to fill gaps.

**4. Cover & Wrap Your foodstuffs.** Make sure you wrap foods properly or put them in sealed containers to prevent the dreaded freezer burn.

**5. Control your portion sizes.** Freeze food in serving-sized portions is the best method. Defrosting a huge stew when all you want is one bowl can be quite a waste.

**6. If in doubt, throw it out.** Unfortunately freezing does not kill bacteria. If you are unsure of how long something has been frozen or are a bit wary of something once defrosted rather avoid eating it, or be prepared to get food poisoning.

**7. Keep it fresh.** Freezing certainly won't improve the quality of your food. Forget about freezing old food because you don't want to waste it; the point of freezing in the first place is to do so when the food in most nutritious and keep it that way.

**8. Organized Labels.** It may seem a bother at the time, but unless you label you might not remember what it is, let alone when it was frozen. Buy a blue marker for raw foods and a green marker for cooked foods.Label the food clearly and simply,no need to get fancy. Large-lettered abbreviations work best, for example a large red  P means cooked pork or a blue F means raw fish. Remember toalways add the date it was frozen, as this will help when determining if it is still good to eat.

**9. Defrosting is a must.** An icy freezer is an inefficient one, so make sure you defrost your freezer if ice builds up. Don't worry about the food; most things will remain frozen in the fridge for a couple of hours while the freezer defrosts.

## What Shouldn't I Freeze?

Here is a few examples of what don't do too well when frozen:

- Raw eggs – they will expand and shells will crack.
- Hard-boiled eggs go rubbery.
- Leaves and vegetables with high water content, such as lettuce, cucumber, bean sprouts and radishes, go limp and mushy.
- Certain softer herb varieties, like parsley, basil and chives, go brown.
- Egg-based sauces usually will separate and curdle- mayonnaise being a common culprit.
- Plain yogurt, low-fat cream cheese, single cream and cottage cheese go watery.

## Cooking from Frozen

A few dishes can be cooked straight from frozen. When using this method, use a lower temperature to start with to thaw, then increase the temperature to cook. Foods include:

- *Soups, stews, braises* and *casseroles.*
- *Bakes, gratins* and potato-topped pies.
- Thin fish fillets, small *fish, sausages,* burgers, and seafood if added at the end of a hot dish.

The foods that should never be cooked from frozen are namely, raw poultry, large joints of meat and thick cuts of steak etc.

# But, Why Should I Use a Slow Cooker

What difference does using slow cooker make when making soups, stews and other meals?

One major advantage of using a slow cooker is the fact that it is fully covered meaning that all the nutrients released by your food are retained in the pot and you therefore get most of the nutrition

Additionally, the slow cooking allows for maximum drawing of nutrients from bones for a delicious and gelatinous broth. Not forgetting that it's perhaps the most convenient cooking tool and all you need is to add all the ingredients to your slow cooker and wait for 8-10 hours for your soup or stew.

Further along the book, we are going to look at delicious Slow Cooker soups and stews that will stabilize your blood sugar levels, increase your cognitive abilities, bring balance to our endocrine system and most of all, and torch away the excess weight.

Using a slow cooker is the best way to save time and still prepare a nutritious meal Assemble the meal in the morning, add all ingredients into the Slow Cooker and at the end of the day Viola! , Dinner is ready -- without much mess or many dishes to clean.

By the same token, add one of these delicious breakfast slow cooker preparations before going to bed and wake up to a delightful meal in the morning that can be had as breakfast or brunch.

The device requires only a very small amount electricity to do its work and when compared with a standard oven, a slow cooker uses a lot less energy.

Cooking with a slow cooker can also be an economically smart choice, because you can use cheaper cuts of meat. Condensation acts as a self-baster, so traditionally tougher cuts of meat become tender in a slow cooker.

And just because you're saving time and money doesn't mean you're sacrificing taste. Vegetables cooked in a slow cooker can absorb stocks and spices, giving them fuller flavours.

I hope you enjoy the recipes contained in this book as much as I have enjoyed developing them!

# One Month Meal Plan

You've heard it said; 'failure to plan is planning to fail.' Whether you are only cooking for one or for your entire family, taking the time to sit and plan for what you are going to eat for the coming week will not just save you time, money and effort; it will also enhance your healthy eating habits.

## Four reasons why you should have a meal plan:

- **You will culture healthy eating habits**

The main premise of Freezer Meals Slow Cooker Plan is to eat foods that easily come together and save you lots of time. When you have a carefully set out meal plan, you won't need to resort to ordering takeout as you will have healthy food waiting for you at home.

Habit is second to nature and as you get used to planning healthy meals, you will soon forget about the processed and inflammatory foods that used to slow you down.

- **You become an informed shopper**

The specific ingredients listed in the recipes you are going to make will teach you the healthiest ingredients that you need to buy. Forget about overly processed food that has got no nutritional value, you focus will now shift to fresh, natural, nutrient dense foods.

- **You will save time and money**

When you know exactly what you are going to cook, you will shop for ingredients more efficiently and thus save more money. You won't also have to waste time brainstorming on what to cook as it's already planned.

- **You will eat a variety of food**

Planning your meals will allow you to eat something new almost every day, if not every day, instead of eating one thing all week. If you have a family, they are sure to dig this method and it will give them something to look forward to every day.

| Meal Plan – Week One | | | |
|---|---|---|---|
| | **Monday** | **Tuesday** | **Wednesday** |
| **Breakfast** | Greens and Breakfast Sausage Casseroles | Pumpkin Pie with Almond Meal | Sausage and Peppers Mix Omelet |
| **Lunch** | Curried Chicken | Spicy Red Cabbage with Bacon and Sausages | Hot Roast Beef and Bacon Stew |
| **Dinner** | Catalonian Chicken | Smooth Pork Chops and Bacon | Lamb with Mushrooms Haricot |
| **Thursday** | **Friday** | **Saturday** | **Sunday** |
| Breakfast Mulberries Almond Mash | Slow Cooker Carrot Zucchini Pecans Pie | Crock Pot Sausage, Broccoli & Egg Casserole | Courgette Sausages and Bacon Casserole |
| Smoked Pork Sausage With Shallots (Slow Cooker) | Ground Turkey and Eggplant Braise | Slow Cooker Beefy Cabbage Stew | Hearty Slow Cooker Mince |
| Peppermint Lamb with Green Beans | Creamy Seafood Soup with Bacon | Chorizo & Sweet Potato Soup | Curried Chicken Stew |

| Meal Plan – Week Two | | | |
|---|---|---|---|
| | **Monday** | **Tuesday** | **Wednesday** |
| **Breakfast** | Small Breakfast | Greens and Breakfast Sausage Casseroles | Crock Pot Sausage, Broccoli & Egg Casserole |
| **Lunch** | Soupe a L'oignon | Slow Cooker Ground Beef and Pumpkin Chili | Spicy Turkey Stew |
| **Dinner** | Braised Apple Cider Pork | Creamy Chicken | Seafood Chowder |
| **Thursday** | **Friday** | **Saturday** | **Sunday** |
| Sausage and Peppers Mix Omelet | Chuck Beef Stew | Tasty Pork Cassoulet | Spanish Chorizo Sausages and Chicken Stew |
| Seafood Soup | Oriental Garlicky Chicken Thighs | Pordenone Cauliflower Lasagna | Monterey Jack Steak |
| Hungarian Rhapsody Cabbage Stew | Red Thai Chicken Stew | Chicken & Olive Stew with Almonds | Tomato Bredie |

| Meal Plan – Week Three | | | |
|---|---|---|---|
| | **Monday** | **Tuesday** | **Wednesday** |
| **Breakfast** | Chives and Bacon Breakfast Omelet | Spicy Breakfast Casserole | Brussels Sprouts and Sausage Casseroles |
| **Lunch** | Balsamic Lamb Stew | Spicy Turkey Stew | Smoked Paprika Pork Tenderloin |
| **Dinner** | Farmhouse Lamb & Cabbage Stew | Thai Nut Chicken | Flavorful Beef & Broccoli Stew |
| **Thursday** | **Friday** | **Saturday** | **Sunday** |
| Crock Pot Broccoli and Sausages Breakfast | Slow Cooker Bacon Mushroom Breakfast | Courgette Sausages and Bacon Casserole | Crock Pot Breakfast Pizza |
| Smoked Paprika Pork Tenderloin | Spinach-Feta Stuffed Chicken Breasts | Lobster Bisque | Tasty Pork Cassoulet * |
| Chicken Parikash | Lemon Zest Chicken Stew | Madras Lamb Curry | Triple Fish Rainbow Pie |

| Meal Plan – Week Four | | | |
|---|---|---|---|
| | Monday | Tuesday | Wednesday |
| **Breakfast** | Summer Squash Casserole | Small Low Carb Breakfast | Slow Cooker Bacon Mushroom Breakfast |
| **Lunch** | Spinach-Feta Stuffed Chicken Breasts | Slow Cooker Beef Roast | Seafood Soup |
| **Dinner** | Crock Pot Crowd Pleaser Beef Stew | Cajun Sweet Potato & Chicken Stew | Oxtail Stew |
| Thursday | Friday | Saturday | Sunday |
| Brussels Sprouts and Sausage Casseroles | Crock Pot Broccoli and Sausages Breakfast | Spicy Breakfast Casserole | Chives and Bacon Breakfast Omelet |
| Spanish Chorizo Sausages and Chicken Stew | Chuck Beef Stew | Slow Cooker Shredded Pork | Lobster Bisque |
| Garlic Gnocchi | Easy Everyday Chicken Soup | Delicious Slow Cooker Tomato & Basil Soup | Tasty Clam Chowder |

# Breakfasts Recipes

# Crock Pot Breakfast Pizza

**Ingredients**
12 large eggs
1 1/4 cup frozen spinach
1 oz smoked sausages
1 cup Parmesan Cheese
5 oz Mozzarella Cheese
1 tsp minced garlic
4 Tbs Olive oil
1/4 tsp nutmeg
Salt and pepper to taste

**Directions**
1. Defost spinach in a microwave stove. Set aside.
2. Mix together all of the eggs, olive oil, and spices. Whisk well until everything is combined.
3. Add in parmesan cheese, and spinach.
4. Pour the mixture into your Crock Pot, then sprinkle Mozzarella cheese over the top. Add smoked sausage slices on top.
5. Cover and cook on LOW 4-6 hours.
6. Slice and enjoy.

Servings: 8

Cooking Times
Total Time: 4 hours

**Nutrition Facts (per serving)**
Carbs: 3,5g
Fiber: 1,5g
Protein: 18,14g
Fat: 19g
Calories: 258

# Greens and Breakfast Sausage Casseroles

**Ingredients**
10 eggs
1 1/4 lbs breakfast sausage
1 cup spinach leaves, roughly chopped
2 cup kale (finely chopped)
1 cup arugula (tough lower stalks removed)
1 onion, diced
1/4 cup coconut milk
1/2 Tbsp coconut oil
1 tsp garlic powder
1/4 tsp nutmeg
sea-salt and freshly ground black pepper to taste

**Directions**
1. Grease your Slow Cooker with coconut oil.
2. Layer the chopped sausages on the bottom of your Slow Cooker. Add chopped onions and on the top place all power greens; spinach, arugula, kale.
3. In a big bowl beat eggs with coconut milk. Adjust salt and pepper to taste.
4. Pour egg mixture over sausages and greens. Sprinkle with garlic powder and nutmeg.
5. Cover and cook on LOW 5-7 hours. Serve hot.

Servings: 10

Cooking Times
Total Time: 20 minutes

**Nutrition Facts (per serving)**
Carbs: 5.34g
Fiber: 0,87g
Protein: 12,9g
Fat: 19,75g
Calories: 252

# Crock Pot Sausage, Broccoli & Egg Casserole

**Ingredients**
10 eggs
1 head broccoli, chopped
12 oz sweet sausages of your choice, cooked and sliced
3/4 cup whipping cream
1 cup Cheddar cheese, shredded
2 cloves garlic, minced
salt and pepper to taste
ghee or lard

**Directions**
1. Grease with lard or ghee your Crock Pot well.
2. Layer one half of the broccoli, half of the sausage and half of the cheese into your Crock Pot. Repeat with remaining broccoli, sausage and cheese.
3. In a bowl, whisk eggs with whipping cream, garlic, salt and pepper to taste. Pour over layered ingredients.
4. Cover and cook on LOW for 4 to 5 hours or HIGH for 2 to 3 hours. Ž
5. Serve hot and enjoy!

Servings: 8

Cooking Times
Total Time: 5 hours

**Nutrition Facts (per serving)**
Carbs: 2,5g
Fiber: 0,2g
Protein: 17g
Fat: 22,4g
Calories: 289

# Summer Squash Casserole

**Ingredients**
6 green onions, sliced and divided in half
12 eggs
2 cups summer squash, diced
1 lb  gluten-free sausage, browned & drained
8 oz shredded Cheddar cheese
8 oz shredded Mozzarella cheese
1/2 cup milk
1/2 tsp salt
1/4 tsp pepper
lard or ghee

**Directions**
1.   Grease a large crock pot with lard or ghee.
2.   Place half summer squash cubes into the bottom. Layer in half the cooked sausage, half the cheeses, and half the green onions, then repeat summer squash diced, sausage, and cheese layers.
3.   In a large bowl, whisk together eggs, milk, salt, and pepper, then drizzle over top.
4.   Cook on HIGH for 4 hours, or LOW for 8 hours.
5.   Serve hot.

Servings: 10

Cooking Time: 8 hours

**Nutrition Facts (per serving)**
Carbs: 3,43g
Fiber: 0,51g
Protein: 19,5g
Fat: 17,17g
Calories: 248

# Slow Cooker Carrot Zucchini Pecans Pie

## Ingredients
1 cup almond meal
1 1 cups almond milk
1 cup chopped pecans
1 small carrot, grated
1 small zucchini, peeled and grated
pinch of nutmeg
pinch of ground cloves
1 tsp cinnamon
2 Tbsp Stevia or any sweetener of your choice
1 tsp of pure vanilla extract
pinch of salt
ghee or olive oil for greasing

## Directions
1. Grease the crock of your Slow Cooker.
2. Combine all of the ingredients, except pecans, in the Slow Cooker.
3. Cook on LOW for 6 to 8 hours.
4. Taste and adjust the seasonings, and add more milk, if needed.
5. Top with chopped pecans. Serve and enjoy!

Servings: 4

Cooking Times
Total Time: 8 hours

## Nutrition Facts (per serving)
Carbs: 8,7g
Fiber: 4,42
Protein: 6,02g
Fat: 16.73
Calories: 195

# Chives and Bacon Breakfast Omelet

**Ingredients**
4 slices bacon, already cooked and crumbled
4 stalks chives
2 tsp lard
4 large eggs
1/4 cup. Cheddar Cheese
Salt and pepper to taste

**Directions**
1. Grease with lard your Slow Cooker Add the crumbled bacon, chives and salt and pepper to taste.
2. In a bowl beat eggs with Cheddar Cheese. Pour the egg mixture over the bacon and chives.
3. Close the lid and cook on LOW for 4-6 hours.
4. Before serving, sprinkle with more chopped chives and serve hot.

Servings: 4

Cooking Times
Total Time: 6 hours

**Nutrition Facts (per serving)**
Carbs: 1,7g
Fiber: 0,7g
Protein: 11,5g
Fat: 24g
Calories: 273
Fiber 0,63g 3%

# Courgette Sausages and Bacon Casserole

**Ingredients**
4 courgettes
1 cup bacon, crumbled
1 Italian sausage links (chicken or pork)
1 cups Colby cheese, shredded
1 cups Monterey Jack cheese shredded
1/2 cup coconut milk
salt and pepper to taste
Ghee or lard

**Directions**
1. Grease the bottom of the Slow Cooker with lard or ghee.
2. Layer sliced cougrettes on the bottom of the pot. Sprinkle with crumbled bacon.
3. Combine the two cheeses, and sprinkle over the cougrettes and bacon.
4. Place a sliced sausages over the cheese and season with salt and pepper to taste.
5. Sprinkle with some more cheese.
6. Pour coconut milk over the top.
7. Set your Slow Cooker to HIGH and cook 3-4 hours. Serve hot.

Servings: 6

Cooking Times
Total Time: 4 hours

**Nutrition Facts (per serving)**
Carbs: 7,42g
Fiber: 1,67g
Protein: 17,44g
Fat: 25,26g
Calories: 409

# Spicy Breakfast Casserole

**Ingredients**
10 oz spicy pork sausages
1 cup salsa of your choice
10 eggs
1 cup whipping cream
1 cup Pepper Jack cheese, or cheese of your choice
1/2 tsp garlic powder
1/2 tsp coriander
1 tsp cumin
1 tsp chili powder
1/4 tsp salt
1/4 tsp pepper

**Directions**
1. Grease the bottom of your Slow Cooker. Place the spicy pork sausages, seasonings and salsa.
2. In a bowl whisk the eggs and whipping cream. Pour the egg mixture over the sausages. At the end add the cheese and stir to combine.
3. Cover and cook on high 2 1/2 hours or LOW 5 hours. Serve hot.

Servings: 10

Cooking Times
Total Time: 5 hours and 15 minutes

**Nutrition Facts (per serving)**
Carbs: 3,62g
Fiber: 0,6g
Protein: 14,42g
Fat: 25g
Calories: 296

# Breakfast Mulberries Almond Mash

### Ingredients
1 cup almond meal
3/4 cup mulberries
2 cups  almond milk
1 Tbs organic honey
1-1/2 Tbs butter, optional
1/2 tsp almond extract
1 Tbs ground flax seed
1/4 tsp salt
coconut butter

### Directions
1. Coat inside of your Slow cooker with cooking spray.
2. Add all ingredients to slow cooker. Stir, cover, and cook on LOW for 7 hours.
3. Spoon oatmeal into bowls; add optional toppings, if desired.
4. Serve.

Servings: 8

Cooking Times
Total Time: 7 hours

### Nutrition Facts (per serving)
Carbs: 16,34g
Fiber:7,63g
Protein: 2,42g
Fat: 3,98g
Calories: 107

# Slow Cooker Bacon Mushroom Breakfast

### Ingredients
6 cooked, drained, crumbled bacon slices
2 cups organic chicken broth
1 cup chopped red bell pepper
1/2 cup Parmesan cheese
1 cups heavy white cream
2 cups sliced, raw mushrooms
2 cups cooked ground sausage
1/2 cup chopped onion
1 Tbs dried parsley
1 tsp garlic powder
1 tsp thyme
salt and pepper to taste

### Directions
1. Add all ingredients to a large Slow Cooker.
2. Cook on LOW mode for 4-6 hour. Make sure not to overcook or cook at too high a heat or the cream will separate. Serve hot.

Servings: 14

Cooking Times
Total Time: 6 hours

### Nutrition Facts (per serving)
Carbs: 2,14g
Fiber: 0,31g
Protein: 6,73g
Fat: 15,52g
Calories: 166

# Crock Pot Broccoli and Sausages Breakfast

### Ingredients
2 cups broccoli florets
10 oz breakfast sausages, pre-cooked, sliced
8 eggs
1 cup Cheddar Cheese, shredded
1 onion, diced
1 cup coconut milk
1 tsp dry mustard
salt and pepper to taste
lard or butter

### Directions
1. Grease or coat a 6 quart slow cooker with lard or butter.
2. In a bowl, beat together the eggs, milk, dry mustard, salt, and pepper to taste.
3. Place the broccoli florets in the bottom of the slow cooker, and top with the onion slices. Season with salt and pepper to taste.
4. 4.At the top place the sausages and the shredded cheese. Pour in the egg mixture over.
5. Cook on LOW for 5-7 hours. Serve hot.

Servings: 6

Cooking Times
Total Time: 6 hours

### Nutrition Facts (per serving)
Carbs: 8g
Fiber: 2.25g
Protein: 18.33
Fat: 16g
Calories: 272

# Brussels Sprouts and Sausage Casseroles

**Ingredients**
8 eggs
2 cups Brussels sprouts
2 links Italian sausages, sliced
1/2 cup shredded Cheddar, divide
2 cloves garlic, minced
3/4 cup cream cheese
salt and fresh ground pepper to taste
ghee or lard

**Directions**
1. Grease your Slow cooker with ghee or lard.
2. In a bowl, whisk eggs, cream cheese, garlic, salt and pepper to taste. Combine all well. Pour over layered ingredients.
3. Layer one half of the Brussels sprouts, half of the sausage and half of the cheese into the slow cooker. Repeat with remaining Brussels sprouts, sausage and cheese.
4. Cook on LOW for 4 to 5 hours or HIGH for 2 to 3 hours. Serve hot.

Servings: 6

Cooking Times
Total Time: 4 hours

**Nutrition Facts (per serving)**
Carbs: 6.72g
Fiber: 1.15g
Protein: 18g
Fat: 21,9g
Calories: 289

# Small Breakfast

**Ingredients**
12 eggs
1 lb chorizo sausage
1 small butternut squash
1 small onion
1 cup coconut milk
Ghee/lard for greasing the crockpot

**Directions**
1. In a frying skillet, cook the chorizo sausages. Dice the onion and peel, de-seed, and dice your squash.
2. In a bowl, whip together eggs and coconut milk.
3. Grease the inside of your Slow Cooker.
4. Put in your squash, the sausage/onion mixture, and then the egg/milk mixture. Stir well.
5. Cook on LOW for 8-10 hours.
6. Serve hot and enjoy!

Servings: 8

Cooking Times
Total Time: 8 hours

**Nutrition Facts (per serving)**
Carbs: 6,94g
Fiber: 0,73
Protein: 13,35
Fat: 18,2g
Calories: 243

# Pumpkin Pie with Almond Meal

**Ingredients**
1 1/2 cups almond meal
15 oz pure pumpkin
1 tsp pumpkin pie spice
1 cup Stevia or natural sweetener of your choice
3 eggs
1 1 tsp baking powder
1 1 tsp baking soda
1 tsp ground cinnamon
1/2 tsp ground cloves
4 Tbsp coconut butter
salt to taste

**Directions**
1. Grease your Crock Pot with coconut butter.
2. In a bowl, beat together butter and sweetener. Add in eggs until thoroughly combined. Add in pumpkin. Combine spices, almond flour, baking soda, baking powder, and salt.
3. Add the mixture to the butter mixture. Pour batter into Slow cooker. Cover and cook on HIGH for 3 hours.
4. When ready, let cool for 15 minutes before serving.

Servings: 8

Cooking Times
Total Time: 3 hours 10 minutes

**Nutrition Facts (per serving)**
Carbs: 11g
Fiber: 3.14g
Protein: 7.41g
Fat: 15g
Calories: 277

# Banana Oat-Flax Mush

**Ingredients**

2 medium bananas, quartered

1 cup oatmeal

4 cups of water

1 cup of flax seeds

1 Tbs of pure vanilla extract

1 Tbs of cinnamon

1 tsp of sea salt

**Directions**

1. Place the whole bananas and remaining ingredients in your Slow Cooker.
2. Set on HIGH and cook for 3 hours.
3. When ready, smash the bananas and mix all well.Let cool and store in the fridge.
4. Serve with milk or your favorite fruits.

**Cooking Times**

Total Time: 3 hours and 5 minutes

**Nutrition Facts (per serving)**

Carbs: 21,39g

Fiber: 7,46

Protein: 4,27g

Fat: 3,31g

Calories: 156

# Sausage and Peppers Mix Omelet

**Ingredients**
8 eggs
1/2 lb pork sausage, cooked
1 cup red peppers, diced
green peppers, diced
1 cup yellow peppers, diced
1 cup shredded Cheddar cheese (optional)
1/2 cup chopped green onions
1/4 cup heavy cream
1/2 tsp crushed red pepper flakes
salt and freshly ground black pepper to taste
ghee / butter / coconut oil (optional)

**Directions**
1. Grease and line sides of Slow Cooker with foil.
2. In a bowl, whisk beat eggs, milk cream, pepper flakes, salt and pepper to taste.
3. Layer in a bottom sausages and diced peppers mix.
4. Pour the egg mixture over the the sausages and peppers.
5. Cover and cook on LOW setting 4 to 5 hours, or on HIGH heat for 2 1/2 to 3 hours.
6. When ready, sprinkle with shredded cheese (optional) and green onions over top of casserole.
7. Cover and cook 10 minutes more.
8. Serve hot.

Servings: 8

Cooking Times
Total Time: 4 hours and 20 minutes

**Nutrition Facts (per serving)**
Carbs: 3g
Fiber: 0,5g
Protein: 14,36g
Fat: 19g
Calories: 245

# Lunch Recipes

# Hot Roast Beef and Bacon Stew

**Ingredients**
3 lb beef roast
4 slices bacon strips
2 cups beef broth (or water)
1 cup onion (chopped)
1 cup  tomatoes (ripe, diced)
1/4 tsp thyme
1 Tbs coconut oil
1 tsp basil
2 tsp dried dill weed
2 tsp garlic powder
2 tsp pepper
1 Tbs garlic salt
1 tsp minced garlic
1 Tbs oregano
4 tsp onion powder
4 tsp dried parsley
5 tsp red pepper flakes
2 tsp hot sauce

**Directions**
1. In the bottom of your Slow Cooker place beef roast and bacon strips. Add on the top all other ingredients and stir lightly.Close the lid and cook on LOW for 6-8 hours.
2. Once ready, taste and adjust salt and pepper, or you can add some additional hot sauce to your own liking.

Servings: 12
Cooking Times: 8 hours

**Nutrition Facts (per serving)**
Carbs: 3,64g
Protein: 22,15g
Fat: 28g
Calories: 369

# Freezer Shredded Pork

**Ingredients**
6 lb pork roast
2 Tbs butter
1 onion, chopped
2 Tbs cumin
2 Tbs thyme
2 Tbs Chili powder
4 Tbs minced garlic
1 cup water
salt and black ground pepper to taste

**Directions**
1. Grease your Slow Cooker with butter.
2. At the bottom of the crockpot place chopped onion and garlic.
3. Cut a crisscross pattern into the top of the pork.
4. Mix spices, salt and pepper and rub into meat.
5. Place meat into crockpot and add 1 cup of water
6. Cook on HIGH for 6-8 hours.
7. Serve hot.

Servings: 16
Cooking Times: 8 hours and 15 minutes

**Nutrition Facts (per serving)**
Carbs: 2,76g
Fiber: 0,81g
Protein: 25,6g
Fat: 22,9g
Calories: 343

# Lobster Bisque

### Ingredients

2 lobster tails
1 cup clam juice
1 3/4 cup stewed tomatoes
1 cup mushrooms, sliced
1 cup coconut milk
3 cups water
1 onion, diced
1 large leek, diced
1 Tbsp dried parsley
2 tsp seasoning mix
1 tsp dill

### Directions

1. In a 5 quart Slow Cooker combine all ingredients together. At the end add in lobster tails.
2. Cover and cook on HIGH for 2 hours, or until lobster tails have turned pink and the meat is fork tender.
3. Remove lobster tails from Slow Cooker. Stir in heavy cream.
4. Ladle into dishes, and serve with lemon slices and lobster meat.
5. Serve hot.

Servings: 4
Cooking Times: 2 hours

### Nutrition Facts (per serving)

Carbs: 10,52g
Fiber: 1,21g
Protein: 24,7g
Fat: 24g
Calories: 357

# Spicy Turkey Stew

**Ingredients**
6 turkey things
6 slices of bacon
1 cup coconut water
1 cup Coconut milk, unsweetened
3 Tbsp tomato paste
2 Tbsp butter, unsalted
1 cup chopped onion
1 hot pepper, chopped
1 Tbs thyme, minced, fresh
1 Tbs basil, fresh, minced
2 Tbs garlic, minced
1 Tbs coconut flour
3 Tbs lemon juice
Salt and fresh black pepper, to taste

**Directions**
1. Grease your Slow Cooker with butter.
2. Thinly slice onions and pepper and evenly place them on the bottom of Slow Cooker.
3. Place boneless turkey thighs. Add over the sliced bacon.
4. Add seasonings (thyme, basil, salt, pepper, garlic, coconut flour).
5. Pour over the lemon juice, coconut water, coconut milk and tomato paste.
6. Cook on LOW for 6 hours
7. Stir and breakup turkey.
8. Serve hot.

Servings: 10
Cooking Times: 6 hours and 5 minutes

**Nutrition Facts (per serving)**
Carbs: 5,56g
Fiber: 1,17g
Protein: 42,3
Fat: 14,3g
Calories: 409

# Curried Chicken

**Ingredients**
8 bone-in chicken thighs
2 tbsp. olive oil or coconut oil
6 carrots, cut in 2-inch pieces
1 sweet onion, cut in thin wedges
1 cup unsweetened coconut milk
1/4 cup mild (or hot) curry paste
Toasted almonds, coriander and fresh green or red chili

**Directions**
1. Cook chicken in a pan skin side down, in hot olive oil for 8 minutes, or until browned.
2. Remove from heat; drain and discard fat.
3. In a slow cooker combine carrots and onion.
4. Whisk together half the coconut milk and the curry paste; pour over carrots and onion
5. Place chicken, skin side up on top of vegetables, pour over olive oil from pan.
6. Cover and cook on high for 3.5 to 4 hours or on low for 7 to 8 hours.
7. Remove chicken from slow cooker. Skim off excess fat from sauce in cooker, then stir in remaining coconut milk.
8. Serve stew in bowls. Top each serving with toasted almonds, corianderer, fresh chili and a dollop of yoghurt or crème fraiche.

Servings: 8
Cooking Times: 7 hours

**Nutrition Facts (per serving)**
Carbs: 20g
Calories 321
Protein 14g
Fats 22g

# Balsamic Lamb Stew

### Ingredients
2 tbsp. olive oil or coconut oil
500 g lamb chops, bone in
1 lamb or beef stock cube
2 cups water
1 cabbage, finely chopped
1 onion, sliced
2 carrots, chopped
2 sticks celery, chopped
1 tsp. dried thyme
1 tbsp. balsamic vinegar
1 tbsp. almond flour or psyllium husk

### Directions
1. Set the slow cooker to low.
2. Heat oil in a large frying pan and brown the lamb chops.
3. Add lamb to the slow cooker with remaining ingredients, mix until ingredients are evenly distributed.
4. Cook on low for 6- to hours. Then remove bones from lamb.
5. For thicker a sauce, 30 minutes before serving ladle ¼ cup of the sauce into a small bowl and whisk almond flour into it with a fork. Return mixture to the slow cooker bowl, stir through, and leave for a further 30 minutes.

Servings: 8
Cooking Times: 6 hours

### Nutrition Facts (per serving)
Carbs: 9g
Calories: 180
Protein: 26g
Fats: 4g

# Smoked Pork Sausage With Shallots

**Ingredients**
8 smoked pork sausage
2 cups homemade chicken broth or water
2 Tbsp celery (chopped)
1 Tbsp olive oil
4 shallots (small, chopped finely)
2 Tbsp almond flour
1 Tbsp soy sauce (no wheat, sugars, or colorings)
salt and black ground pepper to taste

**Directions**
1. In a frying pan heat the oil, add the sausages and brown on all sides.
2. Transfer sausages to your Slow cooker.
3. Add the chopped scallions to the frying pan and cook, stirring occasionally, about 5-6 minutes.
4. Stir in the almond flour and cook, stirring, for 2 minutes.
5. Gradually stir in the stock and bring to the boil, stirring continuously.
6. Stir in the chopped pickles, soy sauce and pepper.
7. Transfer mixture to the Slow cooker and cook on LOW for 5-8 hours.
8. Serve hot.

Servings: 8
Cooking Times: 7 hours

**Nutrition Facts (per serving)**
Carbs: 8,9g
Fiber: 1g
Protein: 11g
Fat: 14,17g
Calories: 203

# Chuck Beef Stew

**Ingredients**

1 packet frozen baby carrots
2 medium onions, roughly chopped
1 small cabbage cored, and cut into 8 wedges
8 garlic cloves, peeled and smashed
2 bay leaves
8 pieces of beef chuck with marrow
salt and freshly ground pepper to taste
2 tins diced tomatoes, drained
1 cup chicken stock

**Directions**

1. Place the baby carrots and chopped onions into the bottom of the slow cooker.
2. Layer the cabbage wedges on top.
3. Add crushed garlic cloves and bay leaves
4. Season the beef shanks with salt and pepper (by the way, feel free to be pretty heavy-handed with the S&P).
5. Add beef shanks on top of vegetables.
6. Pour in the diced tomatoes and broth before putting on the lid.
7. Set the slow cooker on low for 9 hours

Servings: 6
Cooking Times: 9 hours

**Nutrition Facts (per serving)**

Carbs: 5g
Calories 234g
Protein 16g
Fats 16g

# Spanish Chorizo Sausages and Chicken Stew

## Ingredients
1 lbs Spanish Chorizo sausages
4 lbs chicken thighs, boneless and skinless
1 cup Heavy Cream
4 cups homemade chicken stock
1 cup tomatoes
2 Tbs garlic, minced
2 Tbs Worcestershire Sauce
2 Tbs Red Hot Sauce of your choice
Garnish with Sour Cream (optional)

## Directions
1. In a frying skillet, brown chorizo sausages.
2. Layer the ingredients into Slow Cooker starting with the chicken thighs and Chorizo sausages.
3. Cook on HIGH for 3 hours
4. Remove the thighs, break apart, and return to the crockpot; cook on LOW for additional 30 minutes.
5. Garnish with Sour Cream and serve.

Servings: 8
Cooking Times: 3 hours and 50 minutes

## Nutrition Facts (per serving)
Carbs: 4,6g
Fiber: 0,5g
Protein: 20g
Fat: 31g
Calories: 423

# Seafood Soup

**Ingredients**

1 lb white fish, such as mackerel, trout, or dorad
3 cups fish broth
2 cups frozen shrimp
1 cup cauliflower florets
1/2 cup carrots
1 cup zucchini (medium, sliced)
1/2 white onion
heart of celery
4 cloves of garlic
1 cup heavy whipping cream
salt and fresh ground pepper to taste

**Directions**

1. Chop up all the vegetables.
2. ube the fish and dump everything except the cream and the shrimp into your Slow Cooker.
3. Cook on LOW for 8-10 hours.
4. About 30 minutes before serving, stir in your cup of cream and the frozen shrimp.
5. Turn your Slow Cooker to HIGH for the last 30 minutes.
6. Serve with a bit of fresh parmesan cheese.

Servings: 6
Cooking Times: 9 hours

**Nutrition Facts (per serving)**
Carbs: 4g
Fiber: 0,6g
Protein: 18g
Fat: 17,15g
Calories: 246

# Hearty Slow Cooker Mince

**Ingredients**
1kg beef mince
2 brown onions, diced
4 cloves garlic, crushed
1 cup tomato paste
2 tbsp. chicken stock powder or 2 Jelly pots
1 tin tomato soup
1 tin diced tomatoes
1/4 cup sweet chilli sauce
1 tbsp. oregano
2 bay leaves
2 cups water
1 cup finely grated carrot
3-4 finely chopped sticks of celery
2 cups finely chopped mushrooms

**Directions**
1. In a frying pan, add the olive oil and heat. Brown the beef and add the onions and garlic. Cook for 2 minutes more.
2. Mix the tomato paste into the pan and cook for another 2 minutes.
3. Pour all of the mixture into the slow cooker and add the rest of the ingredients and stir.
4. Cook on low for 6 hours or high for 3 hours. (Do not ever skip browning the beef in this recipe. I have tried it and it is NOT good.)

Servings: 8
Cooking Times: 6 hours

**Nutrition Facts (per serving)**
Carbs: 8g
Calories: 187
Protein: 27g
Fats: 5.2g

# Tasty Pork Cassoulet

## Ingredients
1 pack bacon, fried and then crumbled
2 cups chopped onion
1 tsp. dried thyme
1/2 tsp. dried rosemary
3 garlic cloves, crushed
1/2 teaspoon salt
1/2 teaspoon freshly ground black pepper
2 cans diced tomatoes, drained
500g boneless pork loin roast, trimmed and cut into 2cm cubes
250g smoked sausage, cut into 1cm cubes
8 teaspoons finely shredded fresh Parmesan cheese
8 teaspoons chopped fresh flat-leaf parsley

## Directions
1. Fry bacon onion, thyme, rosemary, and garlic, then add salt, pepper, and tomatoes; bring to a boil.
2. Remove from heat.
3. Place all ingredients in the slow cooker, alternating the meat with the tomato sauce until finished. Cover and cook on low for 5 hours.
4. Sprinkle with Parmesan cheese and parsley when cooked

Servings: 6

Cooking Times
Total Time: 5 hours

## Nutrition Facts (per serving)
Carbs: 10.8g
Calories: 258
Protein: 27g
Fats: 12.6g

# Spicy Red Cabbage with Bacon and Sausages

**Ingredients**
2 lbs. red cabbage, shredded
5 oz bacon, finely diced
4 1/2 oz spicy dry-cured sausage, diced
1/4 cup extra virgin olive oil
4 cloves garlic, crushed
1/4 cup homemade broth or water
Salt and freshly ground black pepper to taste

**Directions**
1. Finely chop the red cabbage.
2. In a greased (with olive oil) large Slow Cooker add in the shredded cabbage followed by the bacon, sausages and crushed garlic.
3. Pour over the homemade broth and stir.
4. Close the lid and cook on LOW for 4-6 hours.
5. Before serving adjust salt and pepper if needed and serve hot.

Servings: 10

Cooking Times
Total Time: 6 hours

**Nutrition Facts (per serving)**
Carbs: 11,7g
Fiber: 4,6g
Protein: 7,22g
Fat: 11,4g
Calories: 172

# Barbecue Pot Roast

## Ingredients
8 lbs. Beef Shoulder
5 Teaspoons Garlic (diced)
2 Tablespoons Worcestershire Sauce
1 Tablespoon Mustard
Salt
Black pepper
1 Onion
3 Tablespoons Bacon Fat/Butter
4 Tablespoons Vinegar
4 Tablespoons Splenda/preferred sweetener
1 Teaspoon Liquid smoke

## Directions
1. Chop onion and put aside until needed.
2. Use pepper and salt to season beef.
3. Heat butter/fat in a large frying pan and place beef into pot. Sear for 2 minutes on each side then transfer to slow cooker. Use excess grease in frying pan to sauté onions.
4. Add garlic, vinegar, liquid smoke, mustard, Worcestershire sauce and Splenda/sweetener to pan. Mix together until thoroughly combined.
5. Pour mixture all over meat and set cooker on low.
6. Cook for 9 hours. (Time will depend on size of roast, each lb. should be cooked for about an hour)
7. Remove beef from pot and let it sit for 30 minutes.

Servings: 12
Cooking Times: 9 hours 30 minutes

## Nutrition Facts (per serving)
Carbs: 4g
Calories: 701
Protein: 75g
Fat: 22g

# Slow Cooker Pork Carnitas

## Ingredients
2 Tablespoons Bacon Fat/Butter

2 Tablespoons Cumin

2 Tablespoons Chili powder

1 Tablespoon Black pepper

1 cup Water

8lbs. Pork Butt

1 Onion

2 Tablespoons Thyme

1 Tablespoon Salt

4 Tablespoons Garlic-diced

## Directions
1. Use butter/fat to coat slow cooker.
2. Slice onion and use to line the base of slow cooker and then add garlic.
3. Remove excess fat from meat and use knife to score meat in a crisscross pattern.
4. Combine spices and use to coat meat all over.
5. Place pork on top of onions and garlic and pour in water.
6. Set cooker on high and cook for 8 hours until meat is falling apart.
7. Serve.

Servings: 16

## Cooking Times
Total Time: 8 hours 15 minutes

## Nutrition Facts (per serving)
Carbs: 0g

Calories: 265

Protein: 8g

Fat: 9g

# Chicken Tikka Masala

**Ingredients**

1lb. Chicken thighs- without skin or bones
2 Teaspoons Onion powder
Ginger –grated
5 Teaspoons Garam Masala
4 Teaspoons Salt
1 Cup Heavy Cream
Cilantro- chopped
1 ½ lbs. Chicken thighs- with skin and bones
2 Tablespoons Olive Oil
3 Cloves Garlic- diced
3 Tablespoons Tomato paste
2 Teaspoons Smoked Paprika
10 oz. Canned Tomatoes- diced
1 Cup Coconut Milk
1 Teaspoon Guar gum

**Directions**

1. Cube chicken, removing meat from bones.
2. Combine all dry spices and coat chicken then add to slow cooker.
3. Add ginger, tomato paste and tomatoes; mix together to combine and set on low.
4. Cook for 6 hours then add cream, gum and coconut milk; stir together and heat until desired thickness is reached.
5. Slice and serve.

Servings: 5
Cooking Times: 6 hours

**Nutrition Facts (per serving)**
Carbs: 5.8g
Calories: 493
Protein: 26g
Fat: 41.2g

# Braised Oxtails

**Ingredients**
2 Cups Beef Broth
1 Tablespoon Fish Sauce
1 Teaspoon Onion powder
½ Teaspoon Ginger, ground
1 Teaspoon Thyme, dried
½ Teaspoon Guar gum
2 lbs. Oxtails
2 Tablespoons Soy Sauce
3 Tablespoons Tomato paste
1 Teaspoon Garlic, diced
1/3 Cup Butter
Salt
Black pepper

**Directions**
1. Heat broth in a saucepan then add fish sauce, butter, soy sauce and tomato paste.
2. Season oxtail with pepper and salt and place into slow cooker.
3. Pour mixture in saucepan over oxtails and set on low; cook for 7 hours.
4. Take oxtails from sauce and add gum, stir to combine and heat until gravy thickens.
5. Serve oxtails with desired side and gravy.

Servings: 3
Cooking Times: 7 hours

**Nutrition Facts (per serving)**
Carbs: 3.2g
Calories: 433
Protein: 28.3g
Fat: 29.7g

# Slow Cooker Pizza

### Ingredients
¾ lb. lb. Ground beef
15 Oz. Pizza sauce
3 Cups Spinach
¾ lb. Italian sausage- cooked
3 Cups Mozzarella cheese, shredded
16 slices Pepperoni

### *For topping:*
1 Cup Mushrooms, sliced
½ Cup Sweet onion, diced
¼ Cup, artichoke hearts, marinated, chopped
2 Garlic cloves, diced
1 Cup sliced olives
½ Bell pepper, chopped
¼ cup Tomatoes, chopped

### Directions
1. Combine hamburger, onions, sausage and sauce in a bowl.
2. Add ½ of mixture to slow cooker then top with spinach and pepperoni along with toppings.
3. Top with mozzarella cheese and repeat layers ending with cheese.
4. Set cooker on low and cook for 4 hours. Cool and slice.
5. Serve.

Servings: 8
Cooking Times: 4 hours

### Nutrition Facts (per serving)
Carbs: 11.9g
Calories: 487
Protein: 30g
Fat: 37g

# Ground Turkey and Eggplant Braise

## Ingredients
1 1/2 lb ground turkey
1 1/2 lbs eggplant
3 1/2 cups of whole tomatoes
1/2 cup low sodium chicken broth or water
1 onion, diced
4 garlic cloves, minced
1/2 cup Parmesan cheese
Salt and pepper to taste
Olive oil for greasing

## Directions
1. In a non-stick skillet heat oil over medium heat. Add in the ground turkey, onion, garlic, salt, and pepper. Simmer for about 10 minutes.
2. Transfer the browned meat to your Slow Cooker. Add the remaining ingredients and stir together.
3. Cook for 6-8 hours on LOW until the eggplant completely cooked. Just before serving, adjust salt and pepper and serve hot.

Servings: 8
Cooking Times: 8 hours and 10 minutes

## Nutrition Facts (per serving)
Carbs: 10,15g
Fiber: 4,13g
Protein: 21.14
Fat: 8,64g
Calories: 197

# Slow Cooker Beef Roast

## Ingredients
2 lbs round beef roast
2 cups beef broth
1 onion, sliced
6 cloves garlic, minced
1 Tbs dried Italian seasoning
1 tsp red pepper flakes
1/2 cup red wine
Salt and fresh black pepper, to taste

## Directions
1. Season meat evenly with salt and pepper.
2. Add meat with all ingredient to the Slow Cooker.
3. Cook on LOW for 8 hours.
4. After that time, transfer meat on a serving plate and shred easily with a fork.
5. Serve hot.

Servings: 6
Cooking Times: 8 hours and 10 minutes

## Nutrition Facts (per serving)
Carbs: 2,8g
Fiber: 0,51g
Protein: 13g
Fat: 21,54
Calories: 335

# Smoked Paprika Pork Tenderloin

**Ingredients**

1 1/2 lb pork tenderloin
2 Tbs smoked paprika
1/2 cup salsa of your choice
1 cup low sodium chicken broth or water
1 Tbsp oregano
Salt and pepper to taste

**Directions**

1. In a bowl stir together the chicken stock, salsa, paprika, oregano, salt, and pepper.
2. Add the pork to your Slow Cooker.
3. Pour over the sauce and cook on HIGH for 4 hours. S
4. hred the pork with two forks and cook with the top off for an additional 20 minutes on HIGH.
5. Serve hot.

Servings: 4
Cooking Times: 4 hours and 25 minutes

**Nutrition Facts (per serving)**

Carbs: 4.78g
Fiber: 2,18g
Protein: 29g
Fat: 16g
Calories: 388

# Soupe a L'oignon

**Ingredients**

4 sweet onions (Walla Walla or Vidalia), sliced
4 garlic cloves, minced
8 cups vegetable broth (or water)
2 Tbsp butter
1 Tbsp Worcestershire sauce
1 Tbsp balsamic vinegar
2 tsp Stevia
3 Tbsp amaranth flour
2 Tbsp fresh thyme
salt and pepper to taste

**Directions**

1. In your butter greased Slow Cooker add the onions, garlic, butter, sauce, vinegar, Stevia, salt, and pepper.
2. Sautee for 20-25 minutes stirring occasionally.
3. Stir in the amaranth flour and let cook for 5 more minutes. Add the broth or water and thyme.
4. Cook on LOW for 6-8 hours.
5. Laddle in a bowls and serve hot.

Servings: 8
Cooking Times: 7 hours

**Nutrition Facts (per serving)**

Carbs: 22,02g
Fiber: 3,28g
Protein: 4,7g
Fat: 6,24g
Calories: 164

# Spinach-Feta Stuffed Chicken Breasts

**Ingredients**
6 oz chicken breasts, boneless skinless
1/4 cup black olives, sliced
3 cups spinach, finely chopped
1/2 cup roasted red peppers, chopped
1 cup canned artichoke hearts, chopped
3/4 cup Feta cheese
1 tsp dried oregano
1 tsp garlic powder
1 1/2 cups low sodium chicken broth or water
Salt and pepper to taste

**Directions**
1. Season chicken breast with salt and pepper to taste. With a sharp knife, make a deep cut in the center the chicken breasts to create a pocket.
2. In a bowl, mix together roasted red peppers, spinach, artichoke hearts, feta, oregano, and garlic.
3. Stuff the chicken breasts with the spinach mixture.
4. Add the stuffed chockne to the slow cooker. Pour the chicken broth.
5. Close the lid and cook on LOW for 4 hours. Serve hot.

Servings: 6
Cooking Times: 4 hours and 15 minutes

**Nutrition Facts (per serving)**
Carbs: 10,7g
Fiber: 6,1g
Protein: 17,4g
Fat: 6,62g
Calories: 161

# Slow Cooker Beefy Cabbage Stew

**Ingredients**
1 1/2 lb ground beef
2 lbs green cabbage
1/2 cup unsalted butter
1/2 cup water
3 cups pasta sauce
2 cloves garlic (finely minced)
1 tsp fresh parsley (chopped)
Salt and pepper to taste

**Directions**
1. In a food processor, shred quartered cabbage .
2. In a frying pan, melt the butter and add the cabbage, water and salt and pepper to taste. Add the ground beef and brown for 2 minutes.
3. Transfer all ingredients in a Slow Cooker.
4. Cover lid and cook on LOW for 4 hours.
5. When ready, add the pasta sauce and stir. Serve hot.

Servings: 10
Cooking Times: 4 hours

**Nutrition Facts (per serving)**
Carbs: 12,55
Fiber: 3,62g
Protein: 15g
Fat: 23g
Calories: 309

# Slow Cooker Ground Beef and Pumpkin Chili

### Ingredients
2 lbs ground beef
1 can (15 oz) pumpkin puree ((not pumpkin pie mix)
1 Tbsp pumpkin pie spice
3 cups 100% tomato juice (freshly squeezed if possible)
2 tomatoes, diced
1 red bell pepper
1 yellow onion
2 tsp cumin
1 Tbsp chili powder
2 tsp cayenne pepper
ghee or coconut oil

### Directions
1.  Grease a large Slow Cooker with ghee or coconut oil.
2.  Place the ground meat and pumpkin puree on the bottom of Slow Cooker.
3.  Chop all vegetables and place with rest of ingredients over ground meat and pumpkin puree. (do not add salt and pepper!!). Stir slightly.
4.  Close the lid and cook on LOW for 4-6 hours.
5.  Once ready, season chili with salt and pepper to taste and cook on HIGH another 30 minutes.
6.  Serve hot.

Servings: 8
Cooking Time: 1 hour and 20 minutes

### Nutrition Facts (per serving)
Carbs: 9,87g
Fiber: 2,15g
Protein: 21,7g
Fat: 25,24g
Calories: 355

# Poached Lemon Herbed Salmon

**Ingredients**
1 cup White wine- dry
1 Shallot, sliced thin
6 sprigs Italian parsley
1 Teaspoon Kosher salt
Black pepper
2 Cups Water
1 Lemon, sliced thin
1 Bay leaf
1 Teaspoon Peppercorns
2 lbs. Salmon, with skin
Olive oil, salt and lemon wedges for serving

**Directions**
1. Add wine, shallot, Italian parsley, salt, water, lemon slices, bay leaf and peppercorns to slow cooker and mix together.
2. Heat for 30 minutes then use pepper and salt to coat salmon and add to heated liquid with skin side down.
3. Set on low and cook for 45 minutes.
4. Serve with a drizzle of oil, salt and lemon wedges.

Servings: 4-6

**Cooking Times**
Total Time: 45 minutes

**Nutrition Facts (per serving)**
Carbs: 1.9g
Calories: 520
Protein: 46.5g
Fat: 30.5g

# Pork Vindaloo

**Ingredients**

3 Tablespoons Coconut Oil

3 Onions, sliced thin

12 cloves Garlic, diced

½ Teaspoon Turmeric

1 ½ teaspoons Salt

½ Teaspoon Fenugreek seeds

4 lbs. Pork Shoulder, cubed

6 Serrano chiles, diced

1 ½ Teaspoons Indian Red chile, ground

1 Teaspoon Cumin seeds

6 Cloves

15 Black peppercorns

1 Teaspoon Erythritol

1 Tablespoon Vinegar

2 Tablespoons Coriander seeds

½ teaspoon Mustard seeds –brown

3 Cardamom pods – black

Cassia- 1inch

2 Tamarind Paste

**Directions**

1. Heat slow cooker while prepping ingredients.
2. Heat oil in a skillet and add fenugreek seeds, cover pot and cook until seeds stop popping then add onions. Sauté for 8 minutes then transfer to slow cooker.
3. Add pork, serrano chiles, red chile, salt, ginger, turmeric and garlic. Stir to combine and set on low; cook for 3 ½ hours.
4. Place cumin seeds, cloves, peppercorns, erythritol, coriander seeds, mustard seeds, cardamom and cassia in a grinder and grind together. Add spice mixture to pork and combine thoroughly. Cook for 30 minutes more then add vinegar and paste. Serve.

Servings: 6-8

**Cooking Times**: 4 hours 30 minutes

**Nutrition Facts (per serving)**

Carbs: 11.9g

Calories: 830

Protein: 53.7g

Fat: 62.1g

# Bacon Chicken Chowder

**Ingredients**
1 Shallot, diced
2 Celery Ribs, chopped
1 Sweet Onion, sliced thin
2 Cups Chicken broth
8 oz. Cream Cheese
1 Teaspoon Salt
1 Teaspoon Garlic powder
4 Garlic cloves, diced
1 Leek, sliced
Cremini mushrooms, 6 oz., sliced
4 Tablespoons Butter
1 lb. Bacon –cooked and crumbled
1 lb. Chicken breasts
1 Cup Heavy Cream
1 Teaspoon Thyme
1 Teaspoon Garlic powder

**Directions**
1. Set slow cooker to low and allow to heat then add shallot, celery, onion, broth, garlic, leek, mushrooms, 2 tablespoons butter, black pepper and salt. Cook for 60 minutes.
2. Melt remaining butter in a skillet and sear chicken until golden all over.
3. Remove chicken from skillet and put aside until needed. Add cream cheese, thyme, heavy cream and garlic powder to slow cooker. Mix together until thoroughly combined.
4. Cube chicken and add to slow cooker along with bacon and stir together.
5. Cook for 6 hours. Serve.

Servings: 8
**Cooking Times**: 6 hours 30 minutes

**Nutrition Facts (per serving)**
Carbs: 6.4g
Calories: 355
Protein: 21g
Fat: 28g

# Korean Inspired Ribs

**Ingredients**
1/3 Cup Erythritol
2 Garlic cloves, crushed
½ Teaspoon Red pepper, crushed
1 Cabbage -cut in quarters
1 Tablespoon Sesame oil
½ Cup Tamari Sauce- organic
¼ Cup Rice vinegar –no sugar
1 Tablespoon Grated Ginger
4 lbs. Beef short ribs
½ teaspoon Guar gum
4 Stalk Scallions, sliced thin

**Directions**
1. Combine tamari sauce, vinegar, ginger, red pepper, erythritol and garlic.
2. Place ribs into slow cooker and top with mixture.
3. Set on low and cook for 7 hours then add cabbage on top and cook for an additional 30 minutes.
4. Take ribs and cabbage from slow cooker and add gum to gravy. Heat until thickened,
5. Serve ribs and cabbage with gravy.
6. Top with sesame seeds and scallions.

Servings: 8

**Cooking Times**
Total Time: 7 hours 30 minutes

**Nutrition Facts (per serving)**
Carbs: 1.4g
Calories: 609
Protein: 21g
Fat: 56g

# Tangy Orange Chicken

## Ingredients
¼ Cup Coconut Milk
1 Teaspoon Sesame oil, toasted
½ Teaspoon Ginger, grated
½ teaspoon Orange extract
1 ½ lbs Chicken legs
4 Stalks Green onions, chopped
¼ cup Coconut oil, melted
2 Tablespoons Erythritol
1 Teaspoon Tamari sauce
½ teaspoon Sesame seeds, toasted
¼ Teaspoon Fish Sauce
1 Tablespoon Sesame seeds, black

## Directions
1. Combine all ingredients except chicken.
2. Place chicken in slow cooker and cover with sauce.
3. Set on low and cook for 2 hours and 30 minutes.
4. Serve.

Servings: 4

## Cooking Times
Total Time: 2 hours 30 minutes

## Nutrition Facts (per serving)
Carbs: 1.1g
Calories: 491
Protein: 34g
Fat: 32g

# Vegetarian Coconut Curry

**Ingredients**:
Spinach
½ Onion
1 Teaspoon Ginger, diced
2 Teaspoons Soy sauce
½ Cup Coconut cream
1 Cup Broccoli
4 Tablespoons Coconut oil
1 Teaspoon Garlic, diced
2 Teaspoons Fish sauce
1 Tablespoon Red Curry paste

**Directions**
1. Add all ingredients to slow cooker except broccoli and spinach.
2. Set slow cooker on low and cook for 1 hour then add broccoli and spinach and cook for 30 minutes more.
3. Serve.

**Nutrition Facts (per serving)**
Calories 393
Carbs 6.8g
Protein 5.5g
Fats 38.5g

# Thai Curry Peanut Shrimp

**Ingredients**:
Spinach
1 Cup Vegetable Broth
6 Oz. Shrimp, pre-cooked
3 Tablespoons Cilantro, chopped
1 Tablespoon Peanut Butter
Lime juice
1 Teaspoon Garlic, roasted
1 Teaspoon Fish sauce
¼ Teaspoon Xanthan gum
2 Tablespoons Green curry paste
1 Cup Coconut milk
5 Oz. Broccoli
2 Tablespoons Coconut oil
1 Tablespoon Soy sauce
1 Spring Onion, chopped
1 Teaspoon Ginger, diced
½ Teaspoon Turmeric

**Directions**
1. Heat oil in a skillet and sauté spring onion, garlic and ginger.
2. Add curry, soy sauce, peanut butter, turmeric and fish sauce then add coconut milk and broth. Transfer to slow cooker along with shrimp.
3. Set slow cooker on low and cook for 1 hour then add broccoli and cook for 30 minutes more.
4. Add cilantro to slow cooker and gum and cook until sauce thickens. Serve.

**Nutrition Facts (per serving)**
Calories- 455
Carbs- 8.9g
Protein- 27g
Fats- 31.5g

# Chipotle Honey Chicken

**Ingredients:**
2 lbs. Chicken thighs with skin and bones
1 Tablespoon Olive oil
2 Tablespoons Honey
Salt
Black pepper
1 Tablespoon Butter
½ Cup BBQ sauce
2 Tablespoon adobo Sauce

**Directions**
1. Season chicken with pepper and salt.
2. Heat oil and butter in a skillet and cook chicken until skins are crisp. Transfer chicken to slow cooker.
3. Combine adobo sauce, honey and BBQ sauce and pour over chicken.
4. Set slow cooker on low and cook for 6 hours .
5. Serve.

**Nutrition Facts (per serving)**
Calories 256
Carbs 16.3g
Protein 25.9g
Fats 12.8g

# Mexican Chicken

**Ingredients**:
1 Cup Sour cream
14 Oz. Canned tomatoes and green chilies
2 lbs. Chicken breast
½ Cup Chicken broth
Taco seasoning

**Directions**
1. Add all ingredients to slow cooker except chicken.
2. Heat mixture for 15 minutes then add chicken and use sauce to coat.
3. Set slow cooker on low and cook for 6 hours. Serve.

**Nutrition Facts (per serving)**
Calories 262
Carbs 8.3g
Protein 32g
Fats 13g

# Caramelized Onions

**Ingredients**:
4 Tablespoons Butter
Salt
Black pepper
5 Onions, sliced
¼ Cup Coconut aminos

**Directions**
1. Add all ingredients to slow cooker.
2. Set slow cooker on low and cook for 6-8 hours.
3. Serve.

**Nutrition Facts (per serving)**
Calories 48
Carbs 2.68g
Protein 2g
Fats 2g

# Chicken Fajita Soup

**Ingredients:**
1 ½ lbs. Chicken breast
14.5 oz. Canned Tomatoes
1 Bell pepper, orange-diced
6 Oz. Mushrooms, sliced thin
4 Tablespoons Taco mix
1 Tablespoon Garlic salt
4 Cups Chicken broth
1 Bell pepper, yellow-diced
1 Onion, chopped
4 Garlic cloves. Diced
2 Tablespoons Cilantro, chopped

**Directions**
1.  Add all ingredients to slow cooker.
2.  Set slow cooker on low and cook for 6 hours.
3.  Use fork to shred chicken and cook for 30 minutes more.
4.  Serve.

**Nutrition Facts (per serving)**
Calories 73
Carbs 4g
Protein 15g
Fats 13g

# Slow Cooker Zucchini Meatloaf

**Ingredients:**
2 lbs. Ground Beef
1 Cup Zucchini, shredded and squeezed
½ Cup Italian parsley, chopped
3 Tablespoon Balsamic vinegar
2 Tablespoons Onion powder
½ Teaspoon Black pepper
2 Eggs
½ Cup Parmesan cheese, grated
4 Garlic cloves, crushed
1 Tablespoon Oregano
½ Teaspoon Salt
For topping:
2 Tablespoons Italian parsley
¼ Cup Mozzarella cheese
¼ Cup Ketchup, low salt

**Directions**
1. Combine all ingredients for meatloaf together.
2. Use foil to line slow cooker and spray with cooking spray. Shape mixture into a loaf and place into slow cooker.
3. Set slow cooker on low and cook for 6 hours.
4. Top with ketchup then with cheese and parsley. Cook for 5 additional minutes.
5. Serve.

**Nutrition Facts (per serving)**
Calories 385
Carbs 3.4g
Protein 20.7g
Fats 13g

# Slow Cooker Tex Mex Soup

**Ingredients**:
1 lbs. Ground beef
14 oz. Canned Tomatoes, no sugar
¼ Cup Tomato paste, low sugar
1 Red pepper, sliced
2 Garlic cloves, diced
Tabasco
1 Teaspoon Salt
4 Cups Water
7 oz. Chorizo sausage
2 Tomatoes, chopped
2 Green chilies, chopped
1 Onion, chopped
2 Cups Green beans
¼ Cup Ghee
Black pepper
Parsley

**Directions**
1. Melt ghee in a skillet and sauté garlic and onion. Then add chili pepper and red pepper.
2. Add tomatoes, beef and sausage to pot, stir and transfer to slow cooker. Add all remaining ingredients except green beans to slow cooker and stir.
3. Set slow cooker on low and cook for 6 hours.
4. Add green beans and cook for an additional 30 minutes.
5. Serve.

**Nutrition Facts (per serving)**
Calories 371
Carbs 6.4g
Protein 18.4g
Fats 29.2g

# Slow Cooker Red Gazpacho

**Ingredients**:
2 Green peppers, sliced
1 Red onion, chopped
4 Tomatoes
2 Tablespoons Lemon juice
4 Tablespoons Basil, chopped
2 Spring Onions, chopped
Black pepper
1 Red pepper, sliced
2 Avocados, sliced
2 Garlic cloves, diced
2 Tablespoons apple cider
1 Cucumber
1 Teaspoon Salt
1 Cup Olive oil
7 oz. Feta cheese

**Directions**
1. Place peppers onto a baking sheet and roast at 400 F until slightly charred.
2. Place red peppers along with remaining ingredients into slow cooker. Use an immersion blender to mix together.
3. Set slow cooker on low and cook for 4 hours.
4. Serve.

**Nutrition Facts (per serving)**
Calories 528
Carbs 8.5g
Protein 7.5g
Fats 50.8g

# Butternut Squash Bisque

**Ingredients:**
1 Tablespoon Coconut oil
1 Leeks, sliced
3 lbs. Butternut squash, cubed
4 Cups Chicken broth
1 Teaspoon Salt
¼ Cup Pecans, chopped
2 Sweet Onions, chopped
1 Tablespoon Garlic, chopped
1 Apple, chopped
2 Teaspoons Cinnamon
½ Teaspoon Black pepper

**Directions**
1. Add all ingredients to slow cooker except pecans.
2. Set slow cooker on low and cook for 4 hours.
3. Add pecans and stir, cook for 10 minutes.
4. Serve.

**Nutrition Facts (per serving)**
Calories 248
Carbs 21.8g
Protein 2.7g
Fats 18.2g

# Bacon Cheeseburger Soup

**Ingredients:**
5 Bacon slices
2 Tablespoons Butter
½ Teaspoon Garlic powder
2 Teaspoons Brown mustard
½ Teaspoon Salt
½ Teaspoon Red pepper flakes
1 Teaspoon Chili powder
1 Dill pickle, chopped finely
3 Oz. Cream cheese
12 Oz. Ground beef
3 Cups Beef broth
½ Teaspoon Onion powder
1 ½ Teaspoons Black pepper
1 Teaspoon Cumin
2 ½ Tablespoon Tomato paste
1 Cup Cheddar cheese, shredded
½ Cup Heavy cream

**Directions**
1. Heat skillet and cook bacon until crisp. Remove from pot, cool and chop; put aside until needed.
2. Add beef to skillet and cook for 5 minutes until browned all over.
3. Transfer beef to slow cooker along with spices and butter. Stir together then add broth, cheese, tomato paste and pickles.
4. Set cooker to low and cook for 1 hour.
5. Top with cream and bacon. Serve.

**Nutrition Facts (per serving)**
Calories- 572
Carbs- 3.4g
Protein- 23.4g
Fats- 48.6g

# Delicious Bean-less Chili

**Ingredients:**
2 lbs. Beef stew
1 Green Pepper
1/3 Cup Tomato paste
2 Tablespoons Olive oil
1 ½ teaspoons Cumin
2 Teaspoons Garlic, diced
1 Teaspoon Oregano
1 Teaspoon Worcestershire sauce
1 Teaspoon Salt
1 Onion
1 Cup Beef broth
2 Tablespoons Soy sauce
2 Tablespoons Chili powder
2 Teaspoons Fish sauce
2 Teaspoons Paprika
1 Teaspoon Cayenne pepper
1 Teaspoon Black pepper

**Directions**
1. Cut beef into cubes and place half of beef into a processor. Grind stew beef into ground beef.
2. Add ground beef to skillet and cook for 5 minutes until browned all over; transfer to slow cooker.
3. Add cubed beef to skillet and cook for 5 minutes until meat is browned all over, transfer beef to slow cooker.
4. Add onion and green pepper to skillet, sauté for 3 minutes then add spices and stir together. Add all remaining ingredients and mix together; pour all over beef in slow cooker. Set cooker to high and cook for 2 ½ hours.

**Nutrition Facts (per serving)**
Calories 398
Carbs 5.3g
Protein 51.8g
Fats 17.8g

# Brussel Sprouts Au Gratin

**Ingredients:**
¼ Cup Onion, chopped
2 Tablespoons Butter
½ Teaspoon Liquid smoke
6 Oz. Brussels sprouts
1 Teaspoon Garlic, diced
1 Tablespoon Soy sauce
¼ Teaspoon Black pepper
*For cheese sauce:*
½ Cup Heavy cream
¼ Teaspoon Paprika
¼ Teaspoon Black pepper
1 Tablespoon Butter
2 ½ Oz. Cheddar cheese, shredded
¼ Teaspoon Turmeric
1/8 Teaspoon Xanthan gum
***For crust*:**
½ Teaspoon Paprika
3 Tablespoon Parmesan cheese
1 Oz. Pork rinds

**Directions**
1. Remove stems from sprouts and slice into halves. Chop onion and dice garlic.
2. Melt butter in a skillet and add sprouts, cook for 3 minutes then add garlic and onion. Cook for 3 minutes then add liquid smoke and soy sauce.
3. Combine ingredients for sauce and add to sprouts.
4. Transfer mixture to slow cooker.
5. Put ingredients for crust into a processor and pulse until fine. Use mixture to top sprouts in slow cooker.
6. Set cooker on high and cook for 1-2 hours until crust is set and crisp. Serve.

**Nutrition Facts (per serving)**
Calories 303
Carbs 4.5 g
Protein 9.5g
Fats 27.3g

# Creamed Spinach

**Ingredients:**
1 ½ Cups Cheddar cheese
3 Tablespoons Heavy cream
½ Teaspoon Mrs. Dash seasoning
½ Teaspoon Black pepper
7 Cups Spinach
3 Tablespoons Butter
½ Teaspoon Salt

**Directions**
1. Add all ingredients except cheese to slow cooker.
2. Set cooker on high for 1 hour then add cheese, stir and cook for an additional 30 minutes. Serve.

**Nutrition Facts (per serving)**
Calories 260
Carbs 2.8g
Protein 12g
Fats 27.3g

# Sweet Strawberry Jam

**Ingredients:**
8 Oz. Strawberries
2 Tablespoons Chia seeds
¼ Cup Erythritol powder
½ Cup Water

**Directions**
1. Add all ingredients to slow cooker.
2. Set cooker on high for 1 hour then let jam sit in cooker for 30 minutes. Pour into a glass container and refrigerate Serve.

**Nutrition Facts (per serving)**
Calories 260
Carbs 2.8g
Protein 12g
Fats 27.3g

# Spinach Garlic Dip

**Ingredients:**
6 Bacon slices
½ Cup Sour cream
2 ½ Oz. Parmesan cheese, shredded
1 Tablespoon Garlic, roasted
Salt
Black pepper
8 Oz. Cream cheese
5 oz. Spinach
1 ½ Tablespoons Parsley
1 Tablespoon Lemon juice

**Directions**
1. Add all ingredients to slow cooker except Parmesan cheese.
2. Set cooker on low and cook for 1 hour. Stir together and add Parmesan cheese.
3. Serve.

**Nutrition Facts (per serving)**
Calories 300
Carbs 3.5g
Protein 12g
Fats 26.4g

# Slow Cooker Spicy Chili Soup

**Ingredients:**
2 Tablespoons Olive oil
2 Cups Chicken broth
Salt
Black pepper
½ Teaspoon Cumin
1 lb. Chicken thighs
Avocado
Cilantro
1 Teaspoon Coriander seeds
2 Chili peppers, chopped
2 Cups Water
1 Teaspoon Turmeric
4 Tablespoons Tomato paste
2 Tablespoons Butter
2 Oz. Queso fresco
Lime juice

**Directions**
1.  Heat oil in a deep skillet and heat coriander seeds until fragrant then add chili and saute for 1 minute.
2.  Add water and broth and transfer to slow cooker along with chicken.
3.  Add turmeric, cumin, tomato paste, salt and pepper to taste.
4.  Set cooker to low and cook for 1-2 hours until chicken is tender. Add lime juice and butter and stir, heat until butter melts.
5.  Serve topped with cilantro and queso fresco.

**Nutrition Facts (per serving)**
Calories 396
Carbs 5.8g
Protein 28g
Fats 27.8g

# Mozzarella Bacon Meatballs

**Ingredients:**
1 ½ lbs. Ground beef
1 Cup Mozzarella cheese
½ Cup Pork Rinds, crushed
1 Teaspoon Black pepper
½ Teaspoon Onion powder
4 Bacon slices
1 ½ Cups Pesto Sauce
2 Eggs
2 Teaspoons Garlic, diced
½ Teaspoon Salt
2 Tablespoons Olive oil

**Directions**
1. Combine beef, spices, eggs, pork rinds and cheese together in a bowl.
2. Form mixture into 24 meatballs. You may make them larger but the macros will have to be adjusted.
3. Heat oil in a skillet and fry meatballs until they hold firm. Transfer to slow cooker.
4. Add pesto sauce to slow cooker, set to low and cook for 1 hour.
5. Serve.

**Nutrition Facts (per serving)**
Calories 128
Carbs 0.7g
Protein 10.1g
Fats 9.4g

# Italian Stuffed Meatballs

**Ingredients:**
1 ½ lbs. Ground beef
½ Teaspoon Italian seasoning
½ Teaspoon Onion powder
2 Cups Tomato sauce
2 Eggs
½ Cup Mozzarella cheese
Salt
Black pepper
1 Teaspoon Oregano
2 Teaspoons Garlic, diced
3 Tablespoons Flaxmeal
½ Cup Olives, sliced
1 Teaspoon Worcestershire sauce

**Directions**
1. Combine all ingredients except tomato sauce.
2. Form mixture into meatballs.
3. Place meatballs in slow cooker and add tomato sauce.
4. Set cooker to low and cook for 1 hour.
5. Serve.

**Nutrition Facts (per serving)**
Calories 594
Carbs 3.8g
Protein 36.8g
Fats 44.8g

# Pepper jack and Italian Sausage Meatballs

**Ingredients:**
1 ½ lbs. Ground beef
2 Cups Alfredo sauce
5 Pepper jack Cheese Slices
1 Teaspoon Oregano
1 Teaspoon Salt
1 ½ Italian Sausage, spicy
1/3 Cup Pork rinds
2 Eggs
1 Teaspoon Italian seasoning

**Directions**
1. Combine all ingredients except Alfredo sauce.
2. Form mixture into meatballs.
3. Place meatballs in slow cooker and add Alfredo sauce.
4. Set cooker to low and cook for 1 hour.
5. Serve.

**Nutrition Facts (per serving)**
Calories 289
Carbs 1.2g
Protein 20.8g
Fats22.6g

# Dinner Recipes

# Catalonian Chicken

**Ingredients**

4 boneless skinless chicken breasts
1 can (6 oz) organics tomato paste
3/4 cup water
1 cup  olives with pimento
1 tsp paprika
1/2 tsp garlic powder
salt and pepper (per taste)

**Directions**

1. Wash chicken breasts, drain, and season on both sides with salt, pepper, paprika and garlic powder.
2. Place seasoned chicken breasts in crock pot.
3. Mix tomato paste and water together and pour evenly over chicken breasts.
4. Add olives with liquid.
5. Cover and cook on low for 7-9 hours.
6. Serve hot.

Servings: 6

Cooking Times
Cooking Time: 8 hours and 10 minutes

**Nutrition Facts (per serving)**

Carbs:  7.55g
Fiber: 1,5g
Protein: 24g
Fat: 4,3g
Calories: 220

# Chicken & Olive Stew with Almonds

### Ingredients

1 1/2 cups homemade chicken broth, divided

3 lbs chicken, skinned

1 garlic clove, minced

1/2 cup pitted green olives

1 tsp paprika

1 tsp turmeric

1 Tbsp olive oil

1 tsp ground cumin

1 lemon grated

4 Tbsp amaranth flour

1/4 cup sliced almonds, toasted

2 cups cans diced tomatoes, drained

1 onion, sliced

black pepper and kosher salt to taste

### Directions

1. Place in your Slow Cooker all ingredients exept almond.
2. Cover and cook on HIGH for 4 - 6 hours.
3. Remove chicken from slow cooker and leave to cool.
4. Remove meat from bones and return meat to Slow Cooker. Cook on HIGH for 30 minutes more.
5. Before serving, sprinkle with almonds and serve hot.

Servings: 6

Cooking Times
Total Time: 4 hours and 30 minutes

### Nutrition Facts (per serving)

Carbs: 23g
Fiber: 3g
Protein: 13,6g
Fat: 7g
Calories: 209

# Freezer Dense Beef Soup

**Ingredients**
2 lb top round beef roast
8 oz tomato sauce
2 cups beef broth
1 large onion, sliced
3 Tbsp vegetable oil
2 Tbsp amaranth flour
3 Tbsp sweet paprika
Salt and freshly ground black pepper, to taste
Ghee or lard for frying

**Directions**
1. In a skillet or sauté pan, brown meat and onions in the vegetable oil.
2. Transfer the beef and onion mixture to Slow Cooker with beef broth, flour, tomato sauce, paprika, and pepper.
3. Cover and cook on low for 8 to 10 hours, until meat is tender.
4. Serve hot.

Servings: 8

Cooking Times
Total Time: 8 hours and 20 minutes

**Nutrition Facts (per serving)**
Carbs: 4,46g
Fiber: 0,74g
Protein: 21,32g
Fat: 27,5g
Calories: 353

# Seafood Chowder

**Ingredients**
1 lb scallops
1 lb extra large shrimp
1/2 lb crab legs
1 can crushed tomatoes
4 cups homemade vegetable broth or water
3 cloves minced garlic
1 lb cauliflower florets
1/2 cup onion, diced
1 tsp dried basil
1 tsp dried cilantro
1 tsp dried thyme
1 tsp celery salt
1 tsp salt
1 tsp pepper
1 tsp red pepper flakes
pinch cayenne pepper

**Directions**
1. Add all ingredients except seafood to your Slow Cooker.
2. Cover and cook on HIGH for 2-3 hours or LOW for 4-6 hours.
3. Add thawed seafood to slow cooker and return to HIGH heat and cook for 30-60 minutes until seafood is fully cooked through Serve warm.

Servings: 6
Cooking Times: 7 hours

**Nutrition Facts (per serving)**
Carbs: 25g
Fiber: 3,4g
Protein: 18,24g
Fat: 4,48
Calories: 215

# Lamb with Mushrooms Haricot

**Ingredients**
4 lamb shanks
8 oz mushrooms
1 tsp Worcestershire sauce
10 garlic cloves
1/2 cup beef broth
1 3/4 cup diced tomatoes
1 sweet onion, sliced
1 tsp dried oregano
1 tsp dried basil
4 sprigs fresh thyme
1 tsp ground allspice
1 small bay leaf, broken in half
salt, ground black pepper
1 tsp olive oil

**Directions**
1. Spread sliced and separated onion rings on bottom of crockpot Rub lamb shanks with Worcestershire sauce, then sprinkle all over with salt and pepper.
2. Heat a heavy skillet over medium-high heat. Add olive oil and brown the lamb shanks. Place browned lamb shanks, along with any browned bits from the skillet, in the crockpot on top of the onions. Top with whole garlic cloves and mushrooms.
3. In a medium bowl, mix together beef broth, tomatoes, oregano, basil, thyme, allspice, and bay leaf.
4. Pour mixture over the vegetables and lamb shanks.
5. Cook on LOW for 6 to 8 hours or until tender.
6. Taste and adjust seasoning, if necessary. Serve hot.

Servings: 5
Cooking Times: 8 hours

**Nutrition Facts (per serving)**
Carbs: 13g
Fiber: 2,7g
Protein: 20,2g
Fat: 13,7
Calories: 270

# Delicious Beef Stew

**Ingredients**

1kg stewing beef (choose fatty cuts of meat for best results)
3 tbs. olive oil
2 cups beef stock
1 packet streaky bacon – cooked crisp and crumbled
2 cans diced tomatoes – juice drained
2 cups mixed bell peppers – chopped
2 cups mushrooms – quartered
2 ribs celery – chopped
1 large carrot – chopped
1 small onion – chopped
4 large cloves garlic – minced
2 tbs. organic tomato paste
2 tbs. Worcestershire sauce
2 tsp. sea salt
1 ½ tsp. black pepper
1 tsp. garlic powder
1 tsp. onion powder
1 tsp. dried oregano

**Directions**

1. Set slow cooker on low.
2. In a large pan overr medium heat, sear the beef in olive oil, browning on both sides. Transfer to slow cooker.
3. Pour beef stock, bacon,
4. tomatoes, bell peppers, mushrooms, celery, carrot, onion, garlic, tomato paste, Worcestershire sauce, sea salt, black pepper, garlic powder, onion powder, and dried oregano into the slow cooker.
5. Cover and cook on low 6-8 hours.

Servings: 10
Cooking Times: 8 hours

**Nutrition Facts (per serving)**
Calories 280
Carbs 20g
Protein 18g
Fats 6g

# Slow-Cooker Vegetable Soup

**Ingredients**
4 medium turnips, cutted
2 zucchini, sliced
2 cup vegetable broth or water
1 cup chopped carrots
1 cup onion, diced
2 garlic cloves, minced
1 cup tomato juice, fresh
1/2 tsp ground cumin
1/4 tsp crushed red pepper flakes
1/2 cup frozen peas, defrosted
1/2 cup broccoli florets
salt and black ground pepper to taste

**Directions**
1. Combine the carrots, turnips, onion, garlic, broth or water, salt, cumin, and pepper flakes in a 4- to 6-quart Slow Cooker.
2. Cook on LOW for 6 hours, or on high for 3 hours.
3. Add the chopped zucchini and cook 1 hour longer on LOW mode.
4. Serve hot.

Servings: 6

Cooking Times
Total Time: 7 hours and 15 minutes

**Nutrition Facts (per serving)**
Carbs: 26g
Fiber: 8,5g
Protein: 7g
Fat: 2g
Calories: 179

# Triple Fish Rainbow Pie

**Ingredients**
2 fillets smoked haddock
2 fillets salmon, skinless
2 fillets cod, skinless
4 large eggs
2.2 lbs cauliflower
1 cup butter
3/4 cup red onion
2 bay leaves
4 cloves garlic
1 cup heavy whipping cream
1 cup water
1 tsp Dijon mustard
1 tsp ground nutmeg
1 1 cup cheddar cheese, shredded
4 Tbs freshly chopped chives
salt and freshly ground black pepper to taste
fresh parsley for garnish

**Directions**
1. Start by cooking the eggs. Fill a small saucepan with water up to three quarters. Add a good pinch of salt. To get the eggs hard-boiled, you need round 10 minutes.
2. Grease with butter your Slow Cooker and lay the smoked haddock, cod and salmon filets. Add the cauliflower florets, peeled and finely diced onio, bay leaves and cloves.
3. Slice the eggs and place on the top.
4. In one bowl, mix heavy whipping cream, Dijon mustard, ground nutmgs, salt and pepper and shredded cheddar cheese. Pour the cream mixture over the fish and cauliflower. Cover the fish pie with water. On the top sprinkle freshly chopped chives
5. Close the lid and cook on LOW for 4 - 6 hours.
6. Before serving sprinke the fish pie with chopped parsley and serve hot.

Servings: 10
Cooking Time: 6 hours

**Nutrition Facts (per serving)**
Carbs: 7,43g
Fiber: 2,3g
Protein: 21,9g
Fat: 24g
Calories: 374

# Chorizo & Sweet Potato Soup

**Ingredients**
2 cups sweet potatoes, cubed and peeled
4 cups cabbage and carrot coleslaw mix
1 large onion, chopped
500g chorizo halved lengthwise and cut into thick slices
4 cups chicken stock

**Directions**
1. Place potatoes, coleslaw mix, onion, caraway seeds and sausage in slow cooker. Pour stock in pot.
2. Cover; cook on low for 10 - 12 hours or high for 5 - 6 hours.
3. You can also use beef, chicken, or pork sausages in place of chorizo.

Servings: 6

Cooking Times
Total Time: 10 hours

**Nutrition Facts (per serving)**
Calories 329
Carbs 12g
Protein 40g
Fats 12.4g

# Slow Cooker Chicken & Bacon Chowder

**Ingredients**
4 cloves garlic, minced
1 leek, cleaned, trimmed, and sliced
2 ribs celery, diced
1 punnet button mushrooms, sliced
2 medium sweet onion, thinly sliced
4 tbsp. butter
2 cups chicken stock
6 boneless, skinless chicken breasts, butterflied
8 oz. cream cheese
1 cup heavy cream
1 packet streaky bacon – cooked crisp, and crumbled
1 tsp. salt
1 tsp. pepper
1 tsp. garlic powder
1 tsp. thyme

**Directions**
1. Heat slow cooker on low setting, add garlic, leeks, celery, mushrooms, onions, 2 tbs. butter, 1 cup chicken stock, and salt and pepper. Cover, and cook vegetables on low for 1 hour.
2. Pan-sear the chicken breasts in the remaining 2 tbsp. butter until they are browned on both sides. (Chicken will not be fully cooked during this stage.)
3. Add the remaining 1 cup of chicken stock. Using a spatula scrape up any bits of chicken that may be stuck to the pan. Add chicken stock to slow cooker.
4. Add heavy cream, cream cheese, garlic powder, and thyme to slow cooker. Stir well until there are no longer chunks of cream cheese visible.
5. Once chicken has cooled to room temperature, cut into cubes and add to slow cooker, along with bacon. Stir until all ingredients are well combined. Cover and cook on low for 6-8 hours.

**Nutrition Facts (per serving)**
Calories 355
Carbs 6.4g
Protein 21g
Fats 28g

# Lamb & Swiss Card Curry

**Ingredients**

1/3 cup coconut or olive oil
3 yellow onions , chopped
4 cloves garlic , peeled and minced
2cm piece of ginger , peeled and grated
2 tsp. ground cumin
1 1/2 tsp. cayenne pepper
1 1/2 tsp. ground turmeric
2 cups beef stock, high quality
1.5kg leg of lamb, cut into 2cm cubes
Salt
6 cups baby spinach
2 cups plain full-fat yogurt

**Directions**

1. In a large frying pan over medium-high heat, warm oil. Add onions and garlic, and sauté until golden, about 5 minutes. Stir in ginger, cumin, cayenne, and turmeric and sauté until fragrant, or for about 30 seconds.
2. Pour in broth scraping up the browned bits on the bottom. When broth comes to a boil, remove pan from heat.
3. Put lamb in a slow cooker, and sprinkle with 1 tbsp. salt. Add contents of frying pan. Cover and cook on high-heat setting for 4 hours or low-heat setting for 8 hours.
4. Add baby spinach to pot and cook, stirring occasionally, until spinach is wilted, about 5 minutes. Just before serving, stir in 1 1/3 cups yogurt. Season with salt to taste.

Servings: 10
Cooking Times: 8 hours

**Nutrition Facts (per serving)**
Carbs: 5.5g
Calories: 304
Protein: 32.85g
Fats: 16.32g

# Bacon, Chicken & Mushroom Chowder

**Ingredients**

4 cloves garlic – minced
1 leek – cleaned, trimmed, and sliced
2 ribs celery – diced
1 punnet button mushrooms – sliced
2 medium sweet onion – thinly sliced
4 tbsp. butter
2 cups chicken stock
6 boneless, skinless chicken breasts, butterflied
8 oz. cream cheese
1 cup heavy cream
1 packet streaky bacon – cooked crisp, and crumbled
1 tsp. each salt & pepper
1 tsp. garlic powder
1 tsp. thyme

**Directions**

1. Heat slow cooker on low setting, add garlic, leeks, celery, mushrooms, onions, 2 tbs. butter, 1 cup chicken stock, and salt and pepper. Cover, and cook vegetables on low for 1 hour.
2. Pan-sear the chicken breasts in the remaining 2 tbsp. butter until they are browned on both sides. (Chicken will not be fully cooked during this stage.)
3. Add the remaining 1 cup of chicken stock. Using a spatula scrape up any bits of chicken that may be stuck to the pan. Add chicken stock to slow cooker.
4. Add heavy cream, cream cheese, garlic powder, and thyme to slow cooker. Stir well until there are no longer chunks of cream cheese visible.
5. Once chicken has cooled to room temperature, cut into cubes and add to slow cooker, along with bacon. Stir until all ingredients are well combined. Cover and cook slow for 6-8 hours.

Servings: 10
Cooking Times: 8 hours
**Nutrition Facts (per serving)**
Carbs: 6.4g
Calories: 355g
Protein: 21g
Fats: 28g

# Red Thai Chicken Stew

**Ingredients**

2 tablespoons red curry paste

2 cans of coconut milk

2 cups chicken stock

2 tbsp. fish sauce

2 tbsp. Xylitol

2 tbsp. nut butter

6-8 chicken breasts, cut into pieces

1 red bell pepper, seeded and sliced

1 onion, thinly sliced

4-6 large grated carrots

1 heaped tbsp. fresh ginger, minced

1 tbsp. lime juice

Coriander for garnish

**Directions**

1. Mix the curry paste, coconut milk, chicken stock, fish sauce, Xylitol and nut butter in a slow-cooker bowl.
2. Place the chicken breast, red bell pepper, onion, grated carrots and ginger in the slow cooker, cover and cook on high for 4 hours.
3. Add in the mange tout at the end of the cooking time and cook for ½ hour longer. Stir in lime juice and serve with coriander.

Servings: 10

Cooking Times
Total Time: 4 hours

**Nutrition Facts (per serving)**

Carbs: 10.8g

Calories: 258

Protein: 27g

Fat: 12.6g

# Lemon Zest Chicken Stew

**Ingredients**

2 carrots, chopped

2 ribs celery, chopped

1 onion, chopped

20 large green olives

4 cloves garlic, crushed

2 bay leaves

½ tsp. dried oregano

¼ tsp. salt

¼ tsp. pepper

12 boneless skinless chicken thighs

¾ cup chicken stock

¼ cup almond flour or psyllium husk or finely ground chia seeds

2 tbsp. lemon juice

½ cup chopped fresh parsley

Grated zest of 1 lemon

**Directions**

1. In slow cooker, combine carrots, celery, onion, olives, garlic, bay leaves, oregano, salt and pepper.
2. Arrange chicken pieces on top of vegetables. Add broth and ¾ cup water. Cover and cook on low for 5 1/2 to 6 hours or until juices run clear when chicken is pierced. Discard bay leaves.
3. Whisk flour with 1 cup of the cooking liquid until smooth; whisk in lemon juice. Pour mixture into slow cooker; cook, covered, on high until thickened, about 15 minutes.
4. Mix parsley with lemon zest; serve sprinkled over chicken mixture. Enjoy!

**Nutrition Facts (per serving)**

Calories 345

Carbs 31g

Protein 24g

Fats 17g

# Hearty Beef Stew

**Ingredients**
1kg stewing beef
3 tbs. olive oil
2 cups beef stock
1 packet streaky bacon – cooked crisp and crumbled
2 cans diced tomatoes – juice drained
2 cups mixed bell peppers – chopped
2 cups mushrooms – quartered
2 ribs celery – chopped
1 large carrot – chopped
1 small onion – chopped
4 large cloves garlic – minced
2 tbs. organic tomato paste
2 tbs. Worcestershire sauce
2 tsp. sea salt
1 ½ tsp. black pepper
1 tsp. garlic powder
1 tsp. onion powder
1 tsp. dried oregano

**Directions**
1. Set slow cooker on low.
2. In a large pan over medium heat, sear the beef in olive oil, browning on both sides. Transfer to slow cooker.
3. Pour beef stock, bacon, tomatoes, bell peppers, mushrooms, celery, carrot, onion, garlic, tomato paste, Worcestershire sauce, sea salt, black pepper, garlic powder, onion powder, and dried oregano into the slow cooker.
4. Cover and cook on low 6-8 hours.

**Nutrition Facts (per serving)**
Calories 280
Carbs 20g
 Protein 18g
 Fat 6g

# Madras Lamb Curry

**Ingredients**
8 Fatty lamb chops
6 tbsp. Coconut Milk
2 cups water
3 tbsp. Red Curry Paste
2 tbsp. Thai fish sauce
1 tbsp. dried onion flakes
2 tbsp. dried Thai or fresh red chilies
1 tbsp. Xylitol
1 tbsp. ground cumin
1 tbsp. ground coriander
1/8 tsp., ground cloves
1/8 tsp. ground nutmeg
1 tbsp. ground ginger
*To Serve:*
2 tbsp. coconut milk powder
1 tbsp. red curry paste
2 tbsp. Xylitol
1/4 cup cashews, roughly chopped
1/4 cup fresh cilantro, chopped

**Directions**
1. Place the raw lamb chops in a large slow cooker.
2. Add the 6 tbsp. coconut milk, water, 3 tbsp.red curry paste, fish sauce, onion flakes, chilies, 1 tbsp. Xylitol, cumin, coriander, cloves, nutmeg, and ginger. Cover and cook on high for about 5 hours (or low for 8).
3. Just before serving, scoop out the meat to another dish. Then whisk into the sauce the 2 tbsp. coconut milk powder, 1 tbsp. curry paste, 2 tbsp. sweetener, and 1/4 tsp. xanthan gum(if using).
4. Break the meat into pieces and stir into the sauce, along with the chopped cashews. Garnish with chopped coriander before serving

**Nutrition Facts (per serving)**
Calories 190
Carbs 4g
Protein 18g
Fat 11g

# Curried Chicken Stew

## Ingredients

8 bone-in chicken thighs
2 tbsp. olive oil or coconut oil
6 carrots, cut in 2-inch pieces
1 sweet onion, cut in thin wedges
1 cup unsweetened coconut milk
1/4 cup mild (or hot) curry paste
Toasted almonds, coriander and fresh green or red chili

## Directions

1.  Cook chicken in a pan skin side down, in hot olive oil for 8 minutes, or until browned.
2.  Remove from heat; drain and discard fat.
3.  In a slow cooker combine carrots and onion.
4.  Whisk together half the coconut milk and the curry paste; pour over carrots and onion
5.  Place chicken, skin side up on top of vegetables, pour over olive oil from pan.
6.  Cover and cook on high for 3.5 to 4 hours or on low for 7 to 8 hours.
7.  Remove chicken from slow cooker. Skim off excess fat from sauce in cooker, then stir in remaining coconut milk.
8.  Serve stew in bowls. Top each serving with toasted almonds, coriander, fresh chili and a dollop of yoghurt or crème fraiche.

## Nutrition Facts (per serving)

Calories 321
Carbs 20g
Protein 14g
Fats 22g

# Curried Cauliflower & Chicken Stew

**Ingredients**
3 ½ Tbsp. coconut oil
1 bunch fresh mint or coriander leaves, chopped
1 head cauliflower, broken into large florets
freshly ground black pepper
1 ½ tbsp. salt
6 bone-in skinless chicken thighs, about 1.1kg
500ml whole milk plain yoghurt
750ml chicken stock, low-sodium canned
90ml to 130ml prepared red curry paste (depending on heat required)
5-cm piece fresh ginger, minced
6 cloves garlic, minced
1 lemon, cut in wedges

**Directions**
1. Heat the oil; add the garlic and ginger and cook. Add the curry paste and continue to cook. Whisk the broth in the pan; then pour the liquid into a slow cooker. Whisk the yoghurt into the liquid.
2. Season the chicken all over with salt and pepper.
3. Add the chicken and remaining salt to the slow cooker. Cover and cook on high for 6 hours, adding cauliflower about half way through cooking.
4. Scatter freshly torn mint or coriander on top. Serve with a wedge of lemon.

**Nutrition Facts (per serving)**
Calories 343
Carbs 31g
Protein 23g
Fats 15g

# Tomato Bredie

**Ingredients**

1 tablespoon olive oil

8-10 lamb or mutton chops or 1.5kgs of stewing lamb

2 tablespoons almond flour, psyllium husk or finely ground chia seeds

1 large onion, chopped

1.5 kg. fresh tomatoes, finely chopped

1 tsp. salt

1/2 tsp. freshly ground black pepper

2 bay leaves

1 tsp. Xylitol

1 tbsp. white vinegar

1 dash Worcestershire sauce

1 cube beef or lamb stock

**Directions**

1. Heat oil over medium-high heat, in a large heavy-bottomed saucepan.
2. Dredge meat in almond flour and cook in hot oil until well browned.
3. Stir in onions, and cook for about 5 minutes or until soft. Mix in tomatoes.
4. Season with salt, black pepper, white peppercorns, bay leaves, xylitol, vinegar, Worcestershire sauce, and beef bouillon cube.
5. Cover, reduce heat, and simmer for 3-4 hours on low.

**Nutrition Facts (per serving)**

Calories 404

Carbs 52g

 Protein 28g

 Fats 5g

# Farmhouse Lamb & Cabbage Stew

**Ingredients**

2 tbsp. olive oil or coconut oil

500 g lamb chops, bone in

1 lamb or beef stock cube

2 cups water

1 cabbage, finely chopped

1 onion, sliced

2 carrots, chopped

2 sticks celery, chopped

1 tsp. dried thyme

1 tbsp. balsamic vinegar

1 tbsp. almond flour or psyllium husk

**Directions**

1. Set the slow cooker to low.
2. Heat oil in a large frying pan and brown the lamb chops.
3. Add lamb to the slow cooker with remaining ingredients, mix until ingredients are evenly distributed.
4. Cook on low for 6- to hours. Then remove bones from lamb.
5. For thicker a sauce, 30 minutes before serving ladle ¼ cup of the sauce into a small bowl and whisk almond flour into it with a fork. Return mixture to the slow cooker bowl, stir through, and leave for a further 30 minutes.

**Nutrition Facts (per serving)**

Calories 180

Carbs 9g

Protein 26g

Fat 4g

# Slow Cooker Seafood Stew

## Ingredients

1 tablespoon olive oil

2 onions, diced

4 stalks celery, chopped

4 garlic cloves, minced

1 teaspoon dried oregano

1/2 teaspoon ground black pepper

1 tablespoon tomato paste

1 tablespoon flour

3 cups chicken stock

1 can tomato, onion and chili mix

1 -2 cup tomato cocktail juice

4 chicken breasts, cut into bite size pieces

2 packets mixed frozen seafood, you can add extra mussels in at the end

2 peppers (red and green)

1 jalapeno pepper, chopped

1/4cup parsley, chopped

1 teaspoon chili powder

1 pinch cayenne pepper

1 tbsp. butter

## Directions

1. In a large pan heat the olive oil and fry onions and celery
2. Add garlic, oregano, peppercorns.
3. Stir in tomato paste and almond flour and cook another minute.
4. Add chicken stock, tomatoes and tomato juice and bring to a boil. Continue to cook for about 3-5 more minutes. Remove from heat and transfer mixture to slow cooker.
5. Add chicken and stir to combine. Cover and cook on high for 3 hours or low for 6 hours.
6. Stir in mixed bags of frozen and parsley.
7. Cover and cook on high for 30 minutes

## Nutrition Facts (per serving)

Calories 177

Carbs 15g

Protein 21g

Fats 4g

111

# Rosemary Garlic Beef Stew

## Ingredients
4 medium carrots
4 sticks sleeve celery
1 medium onion
2 tbsp. olive oil
4 cloves garlic, minced
750g beef stewing meat (shin or chuck)
Salt and pepper
¼ cup almond flour
2 cups beef stock
2 tbsp. Dijon mustard
1 tbsp. Worcestershire sauce
1 T tbsp. soy sauce
1 tbsp. xylitol
½ tbsp. dried rosemary
½ tsp. thyme

## Directions
1. Dice the onion and slice the carrots and celery.
2. Place the onion, carrots, celery into a large slow cooker.
3. Place the stewing meat in a large bowl and generously
4. Season with salt and pepper. Add the almond flour and toss the meat until it is well coated.
5. Fry the garlic in the hot oil for about one minute, or until soft and fragrant. Add the seasond meat and all the flour from the bottom of the bowl to the pan. Let the beef cook without stirring for a few minutes to allow it to brown on one side. Stir and repeat until most or all sides of the beef pieces are browned.
6. Add the browned beef to the slow cooker and stir to combine with the vegetables.
7. Add the beef stock, Dijon mustard, Worcestershire sauce, soy sauce, xylitol, rosemary, and thyme to the skillet. Stir to combine the ingredients and dissolve the browned bits from the bottom of the skillet.
8. Once everything is dissolved off the bottom of the skillet, pour the sauce over the ingredients in the slow cooker. (Don't worry if the sauce will not cover the contents of the slow cooker, more moisture will be released as it cooks.)

9. Place the lid on the slow cooker and cook on high for four hours. After cooking, remove the lid and stir
10. stew,breaking the beef into smaller pieces as you stir.
11. Taste the stew and adjust the salt if needed.

**Nutrition Facts (per serving)**
Calories 275
Carbs 24g
Protein 22g
Fats 10g

# Spanish Chorizo Soup

**Ingredients**
2 cups sweet potatoes, cubed and peeled
4 cups cabbage and carrot coleslaw mix
1 large onion, chopped
500g chorizo halved lengthwise and cut into thick slices
4 cups chicken stock

**Directions**
1. Place potatoes, coleslaw mix, onion, caraway seeds and sausage in slow cooker. Pour stock in pot.
2. Cover; cook on low for 10 - 12 hours or high for 5 - 6 hours.
3. You can also use beef, chicken, or pork sausages in place chorizo.

**Nutrition Facts (per serving)**
Calories 329
Carbs 12g
Protein 40g
Fats 12.4g

# Crock Pot Crowd Pleaser Beef Stew

**Ingredients**

1kg beef stewing meat, (cut into bite-sized pieces)
1 tsp. Salt
1 tsp. pepper
1 medium onion, finely chopped
2 celery ribs, sliced
2-3 cloves of garlic, minced
1 can tomato paste
1 liter beef stock
2 Tablespoons Worcestershire sauce
2 cups frozen veg
1/4 cup almond flour
1/4 cup water

**Directions**

1. Combine beef, celery, carrots, red onion, potatoes, salt, pepper, garlic, parsley, oregano, Worcestershire sauce, beef broth, and tomato paste in the crock pot.
2. Cook on low for 10 hours or on HIGH for 6-7 hours.
3. About 30 minutes before serving, mix the flour and the water together in a small dish and pour into the crockpot. Mix until well combined. This will add a nice thickness to the stew. Next add in your frozen veg. Continue cooking covered for 30 minutes.

**Nutrition Facts (per serving)**

Calories 173
Carbs 20g
Protein 17g
Fat 4g

# Thai Nut Chicken

**Ingredients**

8 boneless skinless chicken thighs (about 2 pounds)
½ cup coconut flour
3/4 cup creamy nut butter
1/2 cup orange juice
1/4 cup diabetic apricot jam
2 tablespoons sesame oil
2 tablespoons soy sauce
2 tablespoons teriyaki sauce
2 tablespoons hoisin sauce
1 can coconut milk
3/4 cup water
1 cup chopped roasted almonds or any of the other nuts on green list

**Directions**

1. Place coconut flour in a large re-sealable plastic bag.
2. Add chicken, a few pieces at a time, and shake to coat.
3. Transfer to a greased slow cooker.
4. In a small bowl, combine the nut butter, orange juice, jam, oil, soy sauce, teriyaki sauce, hoisin sauce and 3/4 cup coconut milk; pour over chicken. Cover and cook on low for 4-5 hours or until chicken is tender.
5. Sprinkle with nuts before serving

**Nutrition Facts (per serving)**

Calories 363
Carbs 11.6g
Protein 38.7g
Fats 18.15g

# Bouillabaisse Fish Stew

**Ingredients**
1 cup dry white wine juice and zest of 1 orange
2 tbsp. olive oil
1 large onion, diced
2 cloves garlic, minced
1 tsp. dried basil
1/2 tsp. dried thyme
1/2 tsp. salt
1/4 tsp. ground black pepper
4 cups fish stock, chicken stock can also be used
1 can diced tomatoes, drained
1 bay leaf
400g boneless, skinless white fish fillet (ex. cod)
400g prawns peeled and deveined
400g mussels in their shells
Juice of 1/2 lemon
1/4 cup fresh Italian (flat-leaf) parsley

**Directions**
1. Heat the oil in a large pan
2. Add the onion and fry all the vegetables until almost tender
3. Add the garlic, basil, thyme, salt, and pepper
4. Pour the wine and bring to a boil. Add the fish stock, orange zest, tomatoes, and bay leaf and stir to combine.
5. Pour everything into a slow cooker, cover the cooker, and cook on low for 4 to 6 hours.
6. About 30 minutes before serving, turn the cooker to high. Toss the fish and prawns with the lemon juice.
7. Stir into the broth in the cooker, cover, and cook until the fish cooks through, about 20 minutes.
8. Add mussel's right at the end and allow to steam for 20 minutes with the lid on.

**Nutrition Facts (per serving)**
Calories 310
Carbs 4.76g
Protein 3.72g
Fats 30.69g

116

# Thai Fish Curry

### Ingredients
1 tbsp. coconut oil
½ tbsp. green thai curry paste (add more if you like a hotter curry)
8-10 spring onions
2 garlic cloves, crushed
1 Thai red chilli, deseeded if you like, and thinly sliced
1 tsp. turmeric
160ml chicken stock
1½ cups coconut milk
2.5cm piece of fresh ginger, peeled and sliced
2 tsp. Xylitol
Juice of 1 lime, plus extra to taste
1 tsp. fish sauce
700g boneless, skinless white fish, such as cod, hake, halibut cut into large chunks
freshly ground black pepper
chopped coriander leaves, to serve

### Directions
1. Fry Spring onions, garlic and chilies then stir in green Thai Curry Paste and then sprinkle over the turmeric.
2. Add the stock, coconut milk, ginger, Xylitol and juice from a fresh lime and season with pepper. Bring to the boil, stirring to dissolve the paste and xylitol, then pour the mixture into the slow cooker.
3. Cover the cooker with the lid and cook on HIGH for 1 hour until the flavors are well blended. Add the fish sauce, if using, and add a little more xylitol and fresh lime juice, if you like.
4. Switch the cooker to LOW. Add the fish, re-cover and cook until the fish is cooked through and flakes easily.
5. Sprinkle with coriander and lime zest and sliced red chilies.

### Nutrition Facts (per serving)
Calories 312
Carbs 20g
Protein 24g
Fats 15g

# Flavorful Beef & Broccoli Stew

**Ingredients**

1 cup beef stock
1/4 cup soy sauce
1/4 cup oyster sauce
1/4 cup Xylitol
1 tablespoon sesame oil
3 cloves garlic, minced
1kg boneless beef chuck roast and thinly sliced
2 tablespoons almond flour, or psyllium husk.
2 heads broccoli, cut into florets

**Directions**

1.  In a medium bowl, whisk together beef stock, soy sauce, oyster sauce, sugar, sesame oil and garlic.
2.  Place beef into a slow cooker. Add sauce mixture and gently toss to combine. Cover and cook on low heat for 90 minutes.
3.  In a small bowl, whisk together 1/4 cup water and almond flour.
4.  Stir in almond flour mixture and broccoli into the slow cooker. Cover and cook on high heat for an additional 30 minutes.

**Nutrition Facts (per serving)**

Calories 370
Carbs 4.63g
Protein 47.33g
Fat 18.21g

# Creamy Seafood Soup with Bacon

**Ingredients**

2 can (6 oz) clams
3/4 lb cod fillets
1 can (11 oz) clam juice
2 Tbsp green chili pepper, finely chopped
2 zucchini (medium)
4 slices bacon, cut into strips
1 cup heavy cream
1 medium shallot, minced
1/2 tsp dried parsley flakes
1/2 tsp dried thyme
Kosher salt and freshly ground black pepper to taste

**Directions**

1. Place all ingredients in your Slow Cooker (except bacon and dried thyme). Season with salt and pepper to taste.
2. Cook on LOW for 2-4 hours.
3. Adjust the soup with salt and pepper to taste. Ladle soup into bowls and sprinkle each with the chopped bacon and dried thyme.

Servings: 6

Cooking Times
Total Time: 4 hours

**Nutrition Facts (per serving)**
Carbs: 14,9g
Fiber: 1g
Protein: 21,5g
Fat: 26g
Calories: 424

# Crock Pot Pork Chops with Scallions

### Ingredients
6 boneless pork chops
2 cup scallions, finely sliced
1 Tbsp Dijon mustard (the granite)
2 tsp organic honey
1/2 tsp garlic powder
1/2 cup orange juice
1 1/2 Tbsp tomato sauce
salt and freshly ground black pepper, to taste
Vegetable oil or ghee

### Directions
1. Grease a large skillet and brown pork chops.
2. Transfer the pork chops in your Slow cooker and sprinkle with the sliced spring onions.
3. Pour remaining ingredients over the pork chops.
4. Cover and cook on LOW 7 to 9 hours.
5. Serve hot.

Servings: 6

Cooking Times
Total Time: 9 hours

### Nutrition Facts (per serving)
Carbs: 7,2g
Fiber: 1g
Protein: 19,24g
Fat: 3,4g
Calories: 150

# Hungarian Rhapsody Cabbage Stew

**Ingredients**
1 lb boneless skinless chicken thighs
1/2 lb sausage links (pork or chicken, sweet or spicy, or a mix)
3 cups sliced mushrooms
2 cups cabbage, cut into wedges
1 cup carrots
1 cup tapioca starch
1/2 cup onion, chopped
2 cloves garlic
2 cups chicken broth
1 can (6 oz) mushroom soup
salt and black ground pepper to taste

**Directions**
1. In 4- to 5-quart slow cooker, mix all ingredients except broth and soup.
2. In medium bowl, mix broth and soup. Pour over meat and vegetables in Slow Cooker; stir gently until blended.
3. Cover; cook on LOW heat setting 6 to 8 hours.
4. Serve hot.

Servings: 8

Cooking Times
Total Time: 6 hours and 20 minutes

**Nutrition Facts (per serving)**
Carbs: 23g
Fiber: 2,7g
Protein: 22g
Fat: 7,8g
Calories: 252

# Beef Sausage Zucchini Soup

**Ingredients**
1/2 lb beef sausage
2 cup zucchini
1/4 cup grated Parmesan cheese
2 cups homemade broth or water
1 cup tomato juice, freshly squizeed
1/2 cup carrots, sliced
2-3 garlic clove, minced
1 1/2 cups water
1/2 tsp dried Italian seasoning
1 bay leaf
salt and black ground pepper to taste

**Directions**
1. In a skillet cook sausage stirring frequently. Drain.
2. In 3 1/2 or 4-quart slow cooker, combine cooked sausage and all remaining ingredients except zucchini and cheese; stir gently to mix.
3. Cover; cook on LOW setting for 7 to 9 hours.
4. About 30 minutes before serving, remove and discard bay leaf from soup.
5. Ladle soup into individual bowls.
6. Sprinkle with cheese. Serve.

Servings: 7
Cooking Times: 9 hours and 45 minutes

**Nutrition Facts (per serving)**
Carbs: 11,8g
Fiber: 2,5g
Protein: 9,4g
Fat: 12g
Calories: 191

# Beef Soup (Crock Pot)

**Ingredients**
1 1/2 lbs round steak
1 cup zucchini (sliced)
1 cup beef broth, canned
1 cup chopped onions
2 carrots, sliced thinly
1/4 cup fresh tomato sauce
salt and pepper, to taste

**Directions**
1. On the bottom of your Crock Pot, place vegetables and add beef strips.
2. Pour the tomato juice and broth (or water) evenly and cook on LOW 6 to 8 hours.
3. Ready!
4. Serve hot.

Servings: 6

Cooking Times
Total Time: 8 hours

**Nutrition Facts (per serving)**
Carbs: 11g
Fiber: 2,6g
Protein: 21g
Fat: 14,24g
Calories: 269

# Braised Apple Cider Pork

## Ingredients
4 lb boneless pork shoulder roast
2 Tbsp almond butter
2 scallions, sliced
4 cloves garlic, minced
1 Tbs olive oil
1/4 cup apple cider vinegar
2 1/2 cups water
1 bay leaf
1 1/2 tsp Dijon mustard
1 pinch cayenne pepper
1 Tbsp fresh thyme
salt, black pepper

## Directions
1. Heat oil in a large skillet over high heat. Sprinkle pork with salt and black pepper. Sear pork until browned, about 3 minutes per side. Transfer to a Slow Cooker.
2. Using the same skillet, reduce heat to medium; cook shallots, stirring, until they begin to soften, 3 to 4 minutes. Add vinegar and cook, stirring and scraping up any browned bits, until liquid is nearly evaporated.
3. Pour shallot mixture over pork in Slow Cooker. Adjust salt and pepper. Cover and cook on LOW for about 6 hours until it is fork tender. Transfer roast to a plate, cover loosely with foil and set aside.
4. Shred or cut pork into slices and serve with sauce.

Servings: 10
Cooking Times: 6 hours

## Nutrition Facts (per serving)
Carbs: 21g
Protein: 33g
Fat: 26g
Calories: 460

# Peppermint Lamb with Green Beans

## Ingredients

3 lbs lamb leg, bone in
6 cups green beans
1 cup mint leaves, freshly chopped
2 Tbsp ghee or lard
4 cloves garlic
1/2 cup water
Salt and pepper to taste

## Directions

1.  Season lamb with salt and pepper to taste. In a frying pan greased with ghee, place the lamb and fry until golden brown from all sides. Take off the heat and set aside.
2.  In a bowl chop the mint and slice the garlic. Set aside.
3.  Place the lamb in the Slow Cooker and sprinkle with garlic and mint mix. Add half to one cup of water. Cover with a lid and cook on HIGH for 6 hours or low for 10 hours.
4.  After 4 hours of cooking, transfer the lamb to a plate.
5.  Place the green beans into the same Slow Cooker and add the lamb. Cook on HIGH for another 2 hours.
6.  Serve hot.

Servings: 6
Cooking Times: 8 hours and 15 minutes

## Nutrition Facts (per serving)

Carbs: 5,5g
Fiber: 3g
Protein: 28g
Fat: 12,54g
Calories: 367

# Seafood Chowder (Crock Pot)

**Ingredients**

1 lb haddock fillets

1 can (6 oz) chopped clams, undrained

1 lb shrimp, peeled and deveined

1 can (6 oz) crabmeat, drained

1/2 cup vegetable broth

1 cup clam juice

1 cup tomato paste

1 can (6 oz) diced tomato

1 Tbsp vinegar

1 Tbs olive oil

6 cloves garlic, minced

2 medium onions, chopped

3 celery ribs, chopped

2 tsp seasoning of your choice

1 bay leaf

2 Tbs minced fresh parsley

**Directions**

1. Place all ingredients except seafood and fish in an 4- or 5-qt. Crock Pot.
2. Cover and cook on LOW 4-5 hours.
3. Once ready, uncover and stir in seafood.
4. Cook, covered, 20-30 minutes on LOW.
5. Remove bay leaf. Stir in parsley and serve hot.

Servings: 6

Cooking Times: 4 hours and 50 minutes

**Nutrition Facts (per serving)**

Carbs: 19,07g

Fiber: 4,1g

Protein: 29g

Fat: 4,59g

Calories: 239

# Grouper and Shrimp Soup

**Ingredients**
1 lb Grouper fish
3 cups of fish or chicken broth; or water
1 cup heavy whipping cream
2 cups frozen shrimp
1/2 cup  carrots
2 cups cauliflower florets
4 cloves of garlic
1/2 white onion
heart of celery
salt and fresh ground pepper to taste
Parmesan cheese freshly grated

**Directions**
1. Chop up all the vegetables. Cube the fish and dump everything except the cream and the shrimp into your Slow Cooker.
2. Cook on LOW for 8-10 hours
3. .If your veggies are too big for your taste, use an immersion blender to smooth it out.
4. About 30 minutes before serving, stir in your cup of cream and the frozen shrimp.
5. Turn your crockpot toHIGH for the last 30 minutes.
6. Serve hot.

Servings: 6
Cooking Times: 9 hours

**Nutrition Facts (per serving)**
Carbs: 3,11g
Fiber: 0,25g
Protein: 18,41g
Fat: 17g
Calories: 241

# Smooth Pork Chops and Bacon

**Ingredients**
4 bone-in pork chops
4 slices bacon
3 cups low-sodium chicken stock
3/4 cup water
2 tsp minced garlic
1 yellow onion, chopped
2 tsp Worcestershire sauce
2 bay leaves
1 Tbsp cider vinegar
1 tsp dried parsley and celery

**Directions**
1. Grease your Crock Pot with a lard or ghee.
2. Place pork chops and bacon on the bottom. Place all remaining ingredients over pork chops. At the end pour in water.
3. Close the lid and cook on LOW for 4-8 hours.
4. Serve hot with a dash of chopped parsley and celery on the top.

Servings: 6
Cooking Times: 8 hours and 20 minutes

**Nutrition Facts (per serving)**
Carbs: 6,25g
Fiber: 0,3g
Protein: 20g
Fat: 16,55g
Calories: 260,53

# Mediterranean Monkfish Stew

**Ingredients**
3/4 lbs monkfish
3 1/2 cups water or fish stock
3 shallots finely chopped
4 tomatoes peeled, deseed and diced
4 Tbsp extra virgin olive oil
1/2 tsp sweet paprika
4 cloves garlic clove, chopped
2 tsp parsley, chopped
salt and black pepper to taste

**Directions**
1. Clean fish and remove any bones. Cut monkfish in a small cubes.
2. Add all ingredients in a Slow Cooker and the fish on the top. Add the garlic and half of the parsley.
3. Pour in the water or fish stock and add the sweet paprika; cook on LOW for 4-6 hours.
4. Season with salt and black pepper to taste. Serve hot.

Servings: 4

Cooking Times
Total Time: 6 hours and 5 minutes

**Nutrition Facts (per serving)**
Carbs: 3,4g
Fiber: 4,74g
Protein: 4,23
Fat: 2,42g
Calories: 136

# Creamy Chicken

### Ingredients
2 lbs chicken breast
1 cup sour cream
1/2 cup homemade chicken stock or water
1 can (15 oz) diced tomatoes and green chilies
1 batch homemade seasoning of your choice
Lard or ghee for greasing

### Directions
1. Grease your Slow Cooker with a lard or ghee.
2. Place chicken breast on the bottom.
3. Place all remaining ingredients over chicken breast. Season to taste.
4. At the end pour in sour cream.
5. Close the lid and cook on LOW for 6-8 hours.
6. Serve hot with a dash of chopped parsley and celery on the top.

Servings: 6

Cooking Times
Total Time: 6 hours and 5 minutes

### Nutrition Facts (per serving)
Carbs: 3,6g
Fiber: 0g
Protein: 6,6g
Fat: 8.41g
Calories: 115

# Beef with Red Cabbage

**Ingredients**
4 lbs corned beef brisket
1/2 head of red cabbage
3 carrots
3 green onions, cut in wedges
1 cup water
salt and pepper to taste

**Directions**
1. Put all ingredients in order listed except cabbage in slow cooker. If necessary, cut corned beef brisket in half to fit in crockpot.
2. Cover and cook on LOW 8 to 10 hours.
3. Add cabbage wedges to liquid pushing down to moisten turn to HIGH and cook 2 to 3 hours longer. I
4. In the case that your crockpot is too small, cook cabbage separately in boiling salted water and serve with the corned beef and carrots.

Servings: 10

Cooking Times
Total Time: 8 hours and 20 minutes

**Nutrition Facts (per serving)**
Carbs: 6,26g
Fiber: 1,4g
Protein: 27g
Fat: 27g
Calories: 384

# Mussel Stew

**Ingredients**

1kg fresh or frozen, cleaned mussels
3 tbsp. olive oil
4 cloves garlic, minced
1 Large onion, finely diced
1 punnet mushrooms, diced
2 cans diced tomatoes
2 tbsp. oregano
½ tbsp. basil
½ tsp. black pepper
1 tsp. paprika
dash red chili flakes
3/4 cup water

**Directions**

1. Fry onions, garlic, shallots and mushrooms, scrape entire contents of the pan into your crockpot.
2. Add all remaining ingredients to your slow cooker except your mussels. Cook on low for 4-5 hours, or on high for 2-3 hours. You're cooking until your mushrooms are fork tender and until the flavors meld together.
3. Once your mushrooms are cooked and your sauce is done, crank the crockpot up to high. Add cleaned mussels to the pot and secure lid tightly. Cook for 30 more minutes.
4. Ladle your mussels into bowls with plenty of broth.
5. If any mussels didn't open up during cooking, toss those as well

**Nutrition Facts (per serving)**

Calories 228
Carbs 32.1g
Protein 4.69g
Fat 9.94g

# Chicken Parikash

**Ingredients**

3 tbsp. almond or coconut flour
1 kg. pounds skinless, boneless chicken breast,
butterflied and cut into strips
2 cups chopped onion
1 1/4 cups chicken stock1 cup chopped red pepper
1/2 cup grated carrot
2 tbsp. sweet paprika
2 tbsp. minced garlic
1 tsp. salt
1 tsp. freshly ground black pepper
1 punnet mushrooms
1 1/4 cups sour cream or crème fraiche

**Directions**

1. Combine almond flour and chicken in a medium bowl; toss well. Add chicken mixture, chopped
2. onion, and the next 8 ingredients (through mushrooms) to an electric slow cooker. Cover and
3. cook on low for 8 hours.
4. Stir in sour cream.

**Nutrition Facts (per serving)**

Calories 250
Carbs 5.2g
Protein 38g
Fats 7.8g

# Creamy Chicken & Pumpkin Stew

**Ingredients**
600g chicken boneless chicken breast
250ml chicken stock
1 can evaporated milk (Full Cream)
1/3 cup of sour cream or crème fraiche
1 tbsp. minced garlic
½ cup grated mature cheddar cheese
fresh or frozen finely chopped pumpkin
salt and pepper to taste

**Directions**
1. In a crockpot combine all ingredients.
2. Cover and turn crock pot on low. Cook for 4.5 hours on low or until both chicken and pumpkin are cooked and soft.
3. Stir sauce in crock pot prior to serving.

**Nutrition Facts (per serving)**
Calories 321
Carbs 17.38g
Protein 35.4g
Fat 12g

# Cajun Sweet Potato & Chicken Stew

**Ingredients**
2 cups cubed sweet potatoes
4 boneless chicken breasts
4 boneless chicken thighs
2 cups chicken stock
1 ½ cups chopped green sweet peppers
1 ¼ cup diced fresh tomatoes
¾ cup can tomatoes, onion and chili mix
1 tbsp. Cajun or curry seasoning
2 cloves garlic, minced
¼ cup creamy nut
fresh coriander
chopped roasted nuts

**Directions**
1. In a slow cooker sweet potatoes, chicken, broth, peppers, diced tomatoes, tomatoes and green chilies mix, Cajun seasoning, and garlic.
2. Cover and cook on low-heat setting for 10 to 12 hours or on high-heat setting for 5 to 6 hours.
3. Remove 1 cup hot liquid from cooker. Whisk the liquid with nut butter in a bowl. Add mixture in cooker.
4. Serve topped with cilantro and, if desired, peanuts.

**Nutrition Facts (per serving)**
Calories 399
Carbs 13.5g
Protein 37g
Fats 21g

# Balsamic Pork

**Ingredients**

1 lb. pork roast
1/2 cup balsamic vinegar
1/3 cup honey
2 tsp. fresh rosemary
1/2 tsp. thyme (Dried)
2 bay leaves
2 tsp. salt
1/4 tsp. black pepper

**Directions**

1. Place pork roast in the slow cooker.
2. Mix all ingredients in a bowl and pour over roast.
3. Cook on low for 6-8 hours, or high for 4-6, depending on the size of the roast.
4. Remove the cooked roast from the slow-cooker.
5. Cover and keep warm.
6. Pour the remaining sauce from slow cooker into a saucepan and bring to a boil.
7. Let it reduce by about half.
8. Slice the roast and pour the sauce over top.

**Nutrition Facts (per serving)**

Calories 379
Carbs 32.7g
Protein 35g
Fat 11.45g

# Oxtail Stew

**Ingredients**

1.5kg of oxtail
1 large pack grated cabbage
1 large pack grated carrots
2 large onions
1 large bunch of celery
1 tin of tomatoes
2 jelly stock cubes
2.5 litres of water
1 tbsp. crushed garlic
1 branch rosemary
2 bay leaves

**Directions**

1. Place all ingredients into a slow cooker and cook on medium for 9 hours.
2. Season with salt and pepper
3. Grate 60g cheddar cheese to finish (optional).

**Nutrition Facts (per serving)**

Calories 152
Carbs 5.4g
Protein 16.7g
Fats 7g

# Italian Gnocchi Soup

**Ingredients**

500g ground spicy Italian sausage
1 small onion, diced
2 cloves garlic, minced
4 cups chicken stock or bone broth
1 red medium pepper, diced
1 cup chopped fresh or frozen spinach
½ cup heavy cream
sea salt and freshly cracked black pepper
optional garnish: Parmesan cheese, chopped parsley & crumbled bacon

**Directions**

1. Fry sausage, onion and garlic. Cook until the sausage is completely browned. Stirring occasionally and break up the sausage with a spoon.
2. Add in the bone broth or chicken stock and diced red peppers to the pot and bring the mixture to a simmer.
3. Reduce heat to medium-low and add the spinach and cook for an additional 5 minutes
4. Add gnocchi & cream and stir to combine.
5. Season to taste with salt and pepper.

**Nutrition Facts (per serving)**

Calories 336
Carbs 4.65g
Protein 40g
Fats 17g

# Garlic Gnocchi

## Ingredients
2 cups shredded mozzarella (Low-Moisture Part-Skim)
3 egg yolks
1 tsp. granulated garlic
1 tbsp. olive oil

## Directions
1. Place cheese and garlic in a microwave safe bowl and toss around to combine. Melt cheese in microwave for about 1 to 1.5 minutes.
2. Fold in one egg yolk at a time until a dough-like consistency forms.
3. Portion dough into 4 balls.
4. Chill in refrigerator for at least 10 minutes.
5. Lightly grease a parchment (and your hands — it helps avoid sticking!) and roll out each ball into a 14-15 logs.
6. Slice each log into 1' pieces. (If you like, you can press the tip of a fork onto each piece to get that "gnocchi" look but it's not necessary)
7. In a large pot, bring about a half a gallon of salted water to a boil (like you would for normal pasta). Place all the gnocchi into the pot and cook until they float, about 2-3 minutes. The strain into a colander. (*note: a few of my readers say that have skipped this step and the gnocchi still turns out great!
8. Heat a large non-stick pan on medium-high heat
9. Add a tablespoon of butter and a tablespoon of oil to pan.
10. Add gnocchi and fry each side for about 1-2 minutes, until golden brown.
11. Season with salt and pepper and serve!

## Nutrition Facts (per serving)
Calories 303
Carbs 5.33g
Protein 40g
Fats 13.5

# Loaded Cauliflower Soup

**Ingredients**
3 cups cauliflower, chopped
1½ cups chicken stock
1½ cups water¼ cup milk
¼ teaspoon salt
1 tbsp. butter
3 cloves garlic, minced
3 tablespoons parmesan
1 cup chopped onion
8-10 spring onions
salt to taste
¼ tsp. pepper
1 tbsp. olive oil
½ teaspoon parsley
1 Packet of streaky bacon, chopped, friend crisp and crumbled
1/2 cup shredded cheddar cheese

**Directions**
1. Chop cauliflower into chunks, add all ingredients to a slow cooker and cover and cook on low for 5 hours.
2. Ladle into bowls. Sprinkle with Parmesan cheese and parsley. (Optional: additional bacon, shredded cheese, and sour cream for topping)

**Nutrition Facts (per serving)**
Calories 245
Carbs 21g
Protein 11.7g
Fats 14.3g

# Smoky Pork Cassoulet

**Ingredients**

1 pack bacon, fried and then crumbled

2 cups chopped onion

1 tsp. dried thyme

1/2 tsp. dried rosemary

3 garlic cloves, crushed

1/2 teaspoon salt

1/2 teaspoon freshly ground black pepper

2 cans diced tomatoes, drained

500g boneless pork loin roast, trimmed and cut into 2cm cubes

250g smoked sausage, cut into 1cm cubes

8 teaspoons finely shredded fresh Parmesan cheese

8 teaspoons chopped fresh flat-leaf parsley

**Directions**

1. Fry bacon onion, thyme, rosemary, and garlic, then add salt, pepper, and tomatoes; bring to a boil
2. Remove from heat.
3. Place all ingredients in the slow cooker, alternating the meat with the tomato sauce until finished. Cover and cook on low for 5 hours. Sprinkle with Parmesan cheese and parsley when cooked

**Nutrition Facts (per serving)**

Calories 258

Carbs 10.8g

Protein 27g

Fats 12.6g

# Delicious French Onion Soup

**Ingredients**
1/4 cup unsalted butter
6 thyme sprigs
1 bay leaf
5 pounds large sweet onions, vertically sliced (about 16 cups)
1 tablespoon sugar
6 cups low-sodium beef stock
2 tablespoons red wine vinegar
1 1/2 teaspoons kosher salt
1 teaspoon black pepper
5 ounces Gruyere cheese, shredded (about 1 1/4 cups)

**Directions**
1. Place butter, thyme, and bay leaf in the bottom of a 6-quart slow cooker. Add onions; sprinkle with sugar. Cover and cook on high for 8 hours.
2. Remove thyme and bay leaf; discard. Add stock, vinegar, salt, and pepper; cook, covered, on HIGH for 30 minutes.

**Nutrition Facts (per serving)**
Calories 258
Carbs 10.8g
Protein 27g
Fats 12.6g

# Red Thai Chicken Soup

**Ingredients**
2 tablespoons red curry paste
2 cans of coconut milk
2 cups chicken stock
2 tbsp. fish sauce
2 tbsp. Xylitol
2 tbsp. nut butter
6-8 chicken breasts, cut into pieces
1 red bell pepper, seeded and sliced
1 onion, thinly sliced
4-6 large grated carrots
1 heaped tbsp. fresh ginger, minced
1 tbsp. lime juice
Coriander for garnish

**Directions**
1.  Mix the curry paste, coconut milk, chicken stock, fish sauce, Xylitol and nut butter in a slow-cooker bowl.
2.  Place the chicken breast, red bell pepper, onion, grated carrots and ginger in the slow cooker, cover and cook on high for 4 hours.
3.  Add in the mange tout at the end of the cooking time and cook for ½ hour longer. Stir in lime juice and serve with coriander.

**Nutrition Facts (per serving)**
Calorie 258
Carbs 10.8g
Protein 27g
Fats 12.6g

# Curried Cauliflower Soup

### Ingredients
1 tablespoon olive oil
1 medium spring onion
1 cup cauliflower, steamed
1 cup beef stock
125ml coconut milk
10 cashew nuts
½ teaspoon coriander
½ teaspoon turmeric
½ teaspoon cumin
2 tablespoons fresh parsley, finely chopped
salt and pepper, to taste

### Directions
1. Place the cauliflower and onion in a large pot and add chicken stock. Stir in coriander, turmeric, cumin and a pinch of salt. Bring to a boil and let boil for 5 minutes.
2. Remove from heat. Using a hand blender, puree ingredients in the pot until smooth. Stir in the coconut milk. Serve with roasted cashew nuts and top with parsley.

### Nutrition Facts (per serving)
Calories 258
Carbs 10.8g
Protein 27g
Fats 12.6g

# Easy Everyday Chicken Soup

**Ingredients**

3 skinned, bone-in chicken breasts
6 skinned and boned chicken thighs
1 tsp. salt
1/2 tsp. freshly ground pepper
1/2 tsp. chicken spice seasoning
3-4 carrots sliced
4 celery ribs, sliced
1 sweet onion, chopped
2 cans evaporated milk
500ml chicken stock

**Directions**

1. Prepare Chicken: Rub chicken pieces with salt, pepper, and chicken spice seasoning. Place breasts in a slow cooker, top with thighs.
2. Add carrots and next 3 ingredients. Whisk evaporated milk and stock until smooth. Pour soup mixture over vegetables. Cover and cook on high 3 1/2 hours or until chicken shreds easily with a fork. Remove chicken; cool 10 minutes.
3. Debone and shred chicken. Stir chicken into soup-and-vegetable mixture. Cover and cook on HIGH 1 hour or until boiling.

**Nutrition Facts (per serving)**

Calories 282
Carbs 5.6g
Protein 24g
Fats 18g

# Creamy Chicken & Tomato Soup

**Ingredients**
8 frozen skinless boneless chicken breast
2 tbsp. Italian Seasoning
1 tbsp. dried basil
2 cloves garlic, minced
1 large onion, chopped
2 can of coconut milk (full fat), shake before opening can to avoid separation
2 cans diced tomatoes and juice
500ml of chicken stock
1 small can of tomato paste
sea salt and pepper to taste

**Directions**
1.  Put all the above ingredients into the slow cooker, cook for 9 hours on low.
2.  After 9 hours take two forks and shred the chicken, set the slow cooker on warm till ready to serve

**Nutrition Facts (per serving)**
Calories 227
Carbs 6.37g
Protein 30g
Fat 3.8g

# Delicious Slow Cooker Tomato & Basil Soup

**Ingredients**

2 cans diced tomatoes, with juice
1 cup finely diced celery
1 cup finely diced carrots
1 cup finely diced onions
1 tsp. dried oregano or 1 T fresh oregano
1 tbsp. dried basil or 1/4 cup fresh basil
4 cups chicken stock
½ tsp. bay leaf
1 cup Parmesan cheese
½ cup butter
2 cups full cream milk
1 tsp. salt
¼ tsp. black pepper
¼ cup almond flour or ground chia seeds

**Directions**

1. Add tomatoes, celery, carrots, chicken stock, onions, oregano, basil, and bay leaf to a large slow cooker.
2. Cover and cook on low for 5-7 hours, until flavors are blended and vegetables are tender.
3. About 30 minutes before serving, Melt butter over low heat and add almond flour. Stir constantly with a whisk for 5-7 minutes.
4. Slowly stir in 1 cup hot soup. Add another 3 cups and stir until smooth. Add all back into the slow cooker.
5. Stir and add the Parmesan cheese, milk, salt and pepper.
6. Cover and cook on LOW for another 30 minutes or so until ready to serve.

**Nutrition Facts (per serving)**

Calories 269
Carbs 4.86g
Protein 35.71g
Fat 11g

# Beef & Cabbage Stew

### Ingredients
2 tablespoons olive or coconut oil
500g ground beef mince
1/2 large onion, chopped
5 cups chopped cabbage
2 cups water
2 tins tomato puree
4 beef stock cubes
1 1/2 teaspoons ground cumin
1 teaspoon salt
1 teaspoon pepper

### Directions
1. Heat oil in a large pot.
2. Add ground beef and onion, and cook until beef brown and crumbled.
3. Transfer mince with fat to a slow cooker. Add cabbage, water, tomato sauce, bouillon, cumin, salt, and pepper. Stir to dissolve stock cubes and cover.
4. Cook on high setting for 4 hours, or on low setting for 6 to 8 hours. Stir occasionally.

### Nutrition Facts (per serving)
Calories 165
Carbs 13.7g
Protein 11.54g
Fats 8g

# 3 – Ingredient Vegetable Beef Soup

**Ingredients**
500g ground beef mince
500ml tomato-vegetable juice cocktail
2 packages frozen mixed vegetables

**Directions**
1. Place ground beef mince in a slow cooker. Cook over medium-high heat until evenly brown and crumble.
2. Add juice cocktail and mixed vegetables.
3. In a slow cooker oven, simmer for 30 minutes.
4. In a slow cooker, cook 1 hour on High.
5. Then reduce heat to Low and simmer 6 to 8 hours.

**Nutrition Facts (per serving)**
Calories 251
Carbs 13.5g
Protein 21.3g
Fat 12g

# Bacon and Cheese Dip

**Ingredients:**
2 Tablespoons Ghee
1 Jalapeno pepper, chopped
1 Cup Cream cheese
2 Cups Swiss cheese, grated
1 Onion, chopped
8 Bacon slices
2 Cups Sour cream

**Directions**
1. Add all ingredients to slow cooker stir together and set to low.
2. Cook for 1 hour til cheeses are melted, stir until combined. Serve.

**Nutrition Facts (per serving)**
Calories 201
Carbs 2.5g
Protein 8.3g
Fats 18.7g

# Tasty Clam Chowder

**Ingredients**

2 can minced clams in brine
4 slices bacon, cut into small pieces
3 sweet potatoes, peeled and cubed
1 cup chopped onion
1 carrot, grated
1 punnet mushrooms fried in butter and blended finely with a hand blender
1/4 teaspoon ground black pepper
2 cans evaporated milk

**Directions**

1.  In a small bowl, drain the clams and reserve the juice.
2.  Add water to the juice as needed to total 1 3/4 cups liquid. Cover the clams and put in refrigerator for later.
3.  In a slow cooker combine the bacon, sweet potatoes, onion, carrot, mushrooms, ground black pepper, evaporated milk and reserved clam juice with water.
4.  Cover and cook on low setting for 9 to 11 hours or on high setting for 4 to 5 hours. Add the clams and cook on high setting for another hour.

**Nutrition Facts (per serving)**

Calories 206
Carbs 21.42g
Protein 9.24g
Fat 9.56g

# Warming Mushroom Soup

## Ingredients

2 punnets white button mushrooms, cleaned, trimmed, and quartered
1 medium onion, roughly chopped
4 cloves garlic, sliced
7 sprigs thyme, divided
2 small lemons, halved
2 tbsp. olive oil
1 1/2 tbsp. red wine vinegar salt and freshly ground black pepper
1/2 cup dry sherry
2 cups milk
1 cup heavy cream
1/2 cup sour cream
3 cups chicken stock or vegetable stock

## Directions

1. Preheat oven to 190C. Place mushrooms, onions, garlic, and 5 thyme sprigs in a large bowl. Squeeze lemons into the bowl and add the squeezed lemon halves. Add olive oil and vinegar.
2. Season with salt and pepper and toss to coat. Transfer to a foil-lined rimmed baking sheet and spread into an even layer.
3. Roast until mushrooms release liquid, about 15 minutes. Carefully drain liquid into a separate container and reserve. Return mushrooms to oven and continue roasting until browned but still tender, about 30 minutes longer.
4. Remove lemons and thyme sprigs and discard.
5. Transfer mushroom mixture along with drained liquid to the slow cooker. Add sherry, milk, heavy cream, sour cream, and stock, along with remaining 2 thyme sprigs. Stir to combine and cook on low for 6 hours.
6. Discard thyme sprigs. Working in batches, transfer soup to a blender. Set blender to lowest speed and slowly increase speed to high. Blend until desired consistency is reached. Alternatively, blend with a hand blender directly in the slow cooker.

## Nutrition Facts (per serving)

Calories 198
Carbs 15.8g
Protein 5g
Fat 13.2g

# Bacon Seafood Soup

**Ingredients**
12 slices bacon, chopped
2 cloves garlic, minced
6 cups chicken stock
3 stalks celery, diced
2 large carrots, diced
ground black pepper to taste
1/2 teaspoon red pepper flakes, or to taste
2 cups onions
2 cup uncooked prawns, peeled and deveined
500g white fish fillet like Hake or Kingklip, cut into bite-size pieces
1 can evaporated milk

**Directions**
1. Fry bacon in coconut oil or olive oil, add onion and garlic. Transfer mixture to a slow cooker.
2. Pour chicken stock into slow cooker. Add celery, and carrots into the stock. Season with black pepper and red pepper flakes.
3. Set the cooker to High, cover, and cook for 3 hours.
4. Stir prawns and fish into the soup and cook 1 more hour. Stir evaporated milk into chowder, heat thoroughly, and serve.

**Nutrition Facts (per serving)**
Calories 281
Carbs 7.8g
Protein 39g
Fat 9.5g

# Cream of Broccoli & Mushroom Soup

**Ingredients**
1 tbsp. oil
1 onion, chopped
2 packets frozen chopped broccoli, thawed
2 cans cream of celery soup
2 punnets of mushrooms friend in butter and blitzed smooth with a hand blender
1 cup shredded cheddar cheese
2 cans evaporated milk

**Directions**
1. Fry the onion in coconut oil and transfer to the slow cooker.
2. Transfer the drained onion to a slow cooker.
3. Place the broccoli, cream of celery soup, mushrooms, cheddar cheese, and milk into the slow cooker.
4. Cook on low for 3-4 hours or until the broccoli is tender.

**Nutrition Facts (per serving)**
Calories 212
Carbs 36.6g
Protein 10g
Fats 4.7g

# Slow Cooker Beef & Veggie Soup

**Ingredients**

1kg beef chuck or neck
1 can diced tomatoes, undrained
2 medium sweet potatoes, peeled and cubed
2 medium onions, diced
3 celery ribs, sliced
2 carrots, sliced
2 cups pumpkin
3 beef stock cubes
1/2 tsp. salt
1/2 tsp. dried basil
1/2 tsp. dried oregano
1/4 tsp. pepper
3 cups water

**Directions**

1.  In a slow cooker, combine all the ingredients.
2.  Cover and cook on high for 6-8 hours

**Nutrition Facts (per serving)**

Calories 253
Carbs 10g
Protein 23g
Fats 14.5g

# Cream of Carrot Soup

## Ingredients
1 onion, diced
2 stalks celery, diced
1 large sweet potato, diced
8 whole carrots, sliced
1 liter chicken broth stock
1 whole bay leaf
salt and pepper, to taste
4 dashes tabasco (or other hot sauce)
1 cup heavy cream
1 teaspoon parsley

## Directions
1. Add all ingredients (except heavy cream and parsley) to a slow cooker. Cook on low setting for 6-8 hours or until vegetables are tender.
2. Remove bay leaf. Using a hand blender, puree the vegetables. (You may also puree in batches using a standard blender.)
3. Turn the heat up to high and stir in heavy cream and parsley. Check seasoning and adjust to taste. Cook for an additional 15 minutes to allow heavy cream to heat thoroughly.

## Nutrition Facts (per serving)
Calories 356
Carbs 14.7g
Protein 5g
Fat 31.7g

# Cream of Tomato Soup

### Ingredients
2 tbsp. unsalted butter
2 large onion, finely chopped
2 cans diced tomatoes with juice
1 cup chicken stock
1 cup heavy cream, warmed
1/4 tsp. cayenne pepper
salt and pepper to taste

### Directions
1. Melt butter and fry onion in it. Transfer to slow cooker.
2. Stir in tomatoes with juice, stock and 1/2 cup water into cooker. Cover and cook on low until tomatoes are very soft, 5 to 6 hours. Puree with a hand blender, then stir in cream.
3. Season with salt and pepper and serve.

### Nutrition Facts (per serving)
Calories 229
Carbs 6g
Protein 24.9g
Fat 11.5g

# Creamy Zucchini Soup

## Ingredients
1 small onion, minced
4 cups grated zucchini with peel
2 cups chicken stock
1 tsp. salt
1 tsp. dried dill
1/2 tsp. white pepper
2 tbsp. butter, melted
250ml sour cream

## Directions
1. Mix together everything except the sour cream in a greased slow cooker.
2. Cook covered for 2 hours on low.
3. Mix in the sour cream and cook for an additional 10 minutes, or until heated through.

## Nutrition Facts (per serving)
Calories 233
Carbs 3.41g
Protein 34g
Fats 8.5g

# Indian Curried Cauliflower Soup

**Ingredients**
1 head cauliflower
2 cups chicken stock
3 cloves garlic
1 can coconut milk
1 cup plain yogurt
1 tablespoon curry powder
salt and pepper to taste
1/4 cup roasted pine nuts
3/4 teaspoon garam masala
1/2 cup xylitol
1/2 tsp. salt
1 tbsp. water

**Directions**
1.  Cut cauliflower from stalk, place in slow cooker, put chicken stock and garlic in the slow cooker.
2.  Cover and cook until tender, about 2-4 hours on low.
3.  Add coconut milk and yogurt to slow cooker and cook for an additional 1 hour on low, then using a hand blender.
4.  Blend until pureed.
5.  Sprinkle with toasted pine nuts and some fresh mint.

**Nutrition Facts (per serving)**
Calories 219
Carbs 4.13g
Protein 33.7g
Fat 7g

# Broccoli & Blue Cheese Soup

**Ingredients**
2 onion, diced
4 stick celery, sliced
4 leek, sliced (white part only)
2 tbsp. butter
1 liter chicken stock
2 large heads of broccoli, cut into florets
140g (1 1/4 cups) crumbled blue cheese
125ml cream

**Directions**
1. Put all of the ingredients into your slow cooker.
2. Stir to combine.
3. Put the lid on the slow cooker and cook on high for 4 hours (or 8 hours on low).
4. Using a hand blender, blitz the soup until smooth
5. Ladle into bowls and top with extra crumbles of blue cheese (if desired).

**Nutrition Facts (per serving)**
Calories 174
Carbs 12.8g
Protein 7.5g
Fats 10g

# Italian Meatball Zoodle Soup

## Ingredients
32 oz. beef stock
1 medium zucchini – spirals
2 ribs celery – chopped
1 small onion – diced
1 carrot – chopped
1 medium tomato – diced
1 ½ tsp. garlic salt
1 ½ lb. ground beef
½ cup parmesan cheese – shredded
6 cloves garlic – minced
1 egg
4 tbs. fresh parsley – chopped
1 ½ tsp. sea salt
1 ½ tsp. onion powder
1 tsp. italian seasoning
1 tsp. dried oregano
½ tsp. black pepper

## Directions
1. Heat slow cooker on low setting.
2. To the slow cooker, add beef stock, zucchini, celery, onion, carrot, tomato, and garlic salt. Cover.
3. In a large mixing bowl, combine ground beef, Parmesan, garlic, egg, parsley, sea salt, onion powder, oregano, Italian seasoning, and pepper. Mix until all ingredients are well incorporated. Form into approximately 30 meatballs.
4. Heat olive oil in a large skillet over medium-high heat. Once the pan is hot, add meatballs and brown on all sides. No need to worry about cooking them all the way through as they will be going into the slow cooker.
5. Add meatballs to slow cooker, cover and cook for 6 hours.

## Nutrition Facts (per serving)
Calories 352
Carbs 4.5g
Protein 40g
Fat 19g

# Thai Curried Beef

**Ingredients:**
1 lb. Ground beef, lean
2 Garlic cloves, diced
1 Tablespoon Red Curry Paste
1 Teaspoon Lime zest
½ cup Coconut milk, light
1 Leek, thinly sliced
1 Teaspoon Ginger, fresh
1 ½ Cups Tomato Sauce
1 Tablespoon Soy Sauce
2 Teaspoons Lime juice

**Directions**
1. Heat a skillet, grease with cooking spray and add garlic along with beef. Cook until beef is browned and crumbly.
2. Transfer beef to slow cooker along with ginger, tomato sauce, lime zest, leek, red curry and soy sauce.
3. Set on low and cook for 4 hours then add lime juice and coconut milk. Cook for an additional 15 minutes.
4. Serve

**Nutrition Facts (per serving)**
Calories 213
Carbs 10g
Protein 26g
Fats 8g

# Greek Style Stuffed Chicken Breasts

**Ingredients:**
3 cups Spinach, chopped
¼ cup Olives, black, sliced
4 Oz. Feta Cheese, low fat
1 Teaspoon Garlic Powder
Salt
Black pepper
2 lbs. Chicken breasts, skinless and boneless
½ Cup Red Peppers, roasted, chopped
1 Cup Artichokes hearts, diced
1 Teaspoon Oregano, dried
1 ½ Cups Chicken broth, low salt

**Directions**
1. Add artichoke, feta cheese, garlic, spinach, red peppers and oregano to a bowl and mix together until combined.
2. Use black pepper and salt to season chicken then use a knife to make a slice in each breast to create a pocket.
3. Fill chicken breasts with spinach-cheese mixture.
4. Place stuffed chicken into slow cooker with stuffed sides facing up. Carefully pour in chicken broth.
5. Set on low and cook for 4 hours.
6. Serve.

**Nutrition Facts (per serving)**
Calories 222
Carbs 8g
Protein 36g
Fats 7g

# Buttery Chicken

**Ingredients:**
1 Tablespoon Vegetable oil
¼ Cup Onion
2 Teaspoons Lemon juice
1 Tablespoon Ginger, diced
1 Teaspoon Chili powder
1 Bay leaf
¼ Cup Half & half
1 Cup Tomato Sauce
Salt & Black pepper
2 lbs. Chicken breasts, skinless and boneless
1 Shallot, diced
2 Tablespoons Butter
4 Garlic cloves, diced
2 Teaspoons Garam Masala
1 Teaspoon Cumin, ground
¼ Cup Yogurt, plain
¾ Cup Milk, non-fat
2 Teaspoons Cayenne pepper

**Directions**
1. Heat oil in a skillet and sauté onion and shallot for 3 minutes until softened.
2. Add lemon juice, garlic, chili powder, cumin, bay leaf, butter, ginger, garam masala and cayenne pepper. Mix together and cook for 1 minute.
3. Add tomato sauce and stir until thoroughly combined then add yogurt, milk and cream (half and half). Lower heat and cook for 10 minutes. Be sure to stir occasionally to avoid burning.
4. Add pepper and salt to taste and transfer to a blender or use an immersion blender to combine.
5. Place chicken in slow cooker and cover with mixture.
6. Set on low and cook for 4 hours. Serve.

**Nutrition Facts (per serving)**
Calories 265
Carbs 9g
Protein 35g
Fats 9g

# Pork Tenderloin

**Ingredients:**
1 ½ lbs. Pork tenderloin
½ Cup Salsa
1 Tablespoon Oregano
Black pepper
1 cup Chicken broth, low salt
2 Tablespoons Smoked Paprika
½ Teaspoon Salt
2 Tablespoons Butter

**Directions**
1. Combine all ingredients in a bowl except butter and pork.
2. Heat skillet and melt butter then add pork and sear on all sides until browned all over.
3. Transfer pork to slow cooker along with sauce.
4. Set slow cooker on high and cook for 4 hours until pork is falling apart.
5. Shred pork and cook for 20 more minutes until liquid reduces.
6. Serve.

**Nutrition Facts (per serving)**
Calories 240
Carbs 5g
Protein 33g
Fats 8g

# Wine and Coffee Beef

**Ingredients:**
2 ½ lbs. Stewing Beef, cubed
1 Cup Beef Broth
2/3 cup Red Wine
3 Tablespoons Coconut oil
2 Teaspoons Garlic
1 Teaspoon Black pepper
3 Cups Black Coffee
1 ½ Cups Mushrooms, sliced
1 Onion, sliced
2 Tablespoons Capers
1 Teaspoon Salt

**Directions**
1. Heat coconut oil in a skillet until it starts to smoke.
2. Season beef with pepper and salt and add to pot. Brown the meat a little at a time then transfer to slow cooker.
3. Sauté garlic, onions and mushrooms in skillet and add to beef.
4. Combine coffee, wine, capers and broth and pour over beef in slow cooker.
5. Set on high and cook for 3 hours.
6. Serve.

**Nutrition Facts (per serving)**
Calories 504
Carbs 2.7g
Protein 42.5g
Fats 32.2g

# Spiced Pumpkin Stew

**Ingredients:**
3 Cups Chicken broth
4 Tablespoons Butter
2 Garlic cloves, roasted
½ Teaspoon Black pepper
¼ Teaspoon Cinnamon
1/8 Teaspoon Nutmeg
½ Cup Heavy Cream
3 Tablespoons grease (from bacon)
2 Cups Pumpkin, cubed
¼ Onion, chopped
½ Teaspoon Salt
½ Teaspoon Ginger, diced
¼ Teaspoon Coriander
1 Bay leaf
4 Bacon slices

**Directions**
1. Melt butter in a skillet and sauté ginger, garlic and onion then transfer to slow cooker.
2. Add broth, pumpkin and spices to slow cooker, stir and set on low. Cook for 2 hours until pumpkin falls apart.
3. Cook bacon until crisp, take from pot, crumble and put aside until needed.
4. Add bacon grease to soup along with cream and use an immersion blender to blend together.
5. Serve topped with bacon.

**Nutrition Facts (per serving)**
Calories 486
Carbs 7.3g
Protein 5.7g
Fats 48.7g

# Italian Beef

**Ingredients:**
2 ½ lbs.  Beef Roast
1 Onion, sliced
1 Teaspoon Salt
1 Teaspoon Basil
½ Teaspoon Thyme
Red pepper flakes
2 Cups Beef broth
2 Cups Carrots, chopped
4 Garlic cloves, diced
1 Teaspoon Garlic powder
1 Teaspoon Oregano
1/8 Teaspoon Cinnamon
1 ½ cups Tomatoes, crushed
1 Tablespoon Tomato Paste

**Directions**
1. Season beef with spices and add to slow cooker.
2. Add garlic, onion and carrots to pot and combine broth and paste and pour over beef.
3. Set on low and cook for 6 hours.
4. Serve.

**Nutrition Facts (per serving)**
Calories 318
Carbs 1.6g
Protein 39.4g
Fats 15.8g

# Beef Stroganoff Soup

**Ingredients:**
1 ¾ lbs., Sirloin steaks
¼ cup Ghee
1 Onion, chopped
2 Teaspoons Paprika
4 Tablespoons Lemon juice
¼ Cup Parsley, chopped
¼ Teaspoon Black pepper
1 ¼ lbs. Mushrooms, sliced
2 Garlic cloves, diced
5 Cups Beef broth
1 Tablespoon Dijon mustard
1 ½ Cups Sour Cream
1 Teaspoons Salt

**Directions**
1. Slice beef into strips and season with pepper and salt.
2. Heat a skillet and melt half of ghee then add beef to pot and cook for 5 minutes until browned all over; transfer beef to slow cooker.
3. Add leftover ghee to skillet and sauté garlic and onion for 2 minutes then add mushrooms and sauté for an additional 2 minutes.
4. Combine mustard, broth and paprika and add to skillet. Stir together and add to beef in slow cooker.
5. Add lemon juice and set on low for 2 hours. Add sour cream, stir and cook for an additional 15 minutes.
6. Serve.

**Nutrition Facts (per serving)**
Calories 520
Carbs 9.8g
Protein 34.9g
Fats 38.4g

# Kohlrabi and Pork Stew

**Ingredients:**
2 ½ lbs. Pork Shoulder
4 Teaspoons Onion powder
4 Teaspoons Paprika
1 teaspoon Caraway seeds
Black pepper
1 Cup Coconut milk
4 Tablespoons Parsley, chopped
4 Tablespoons Ghee
6 Cups Beef broth
¼ Teaspoon Allspice
2 Teaspoons Salt
4 Kohlrabi, sliced
8 Egg yolks
4 Zucchini, sliced

**Directions**
1. Season beef with spices and add to slow cooker.
2. Add ghee and broth and set on high. Cook for 3 hours.
3. Combine coconut milk and eggs and pour into slow cooker, add veggies and cook for an additional hour or until vegetables are tender. Adjust pepper and salt to taste.
4. Serve.

**Nutrition Facts (per serving)**
Calories 318
Carbs 1.6g
Protein 39.4g
Fats 15.8g

# Celeriac Cauli-Mash

**Ingredients:**
1 ½ lbs. Cauliflower
¼ Cup Ghee
1 Tablespoon Thyme
½ Teaspoon Salt
4 Tablespoons Butter
7 Oz. Celeriac
1 Tablespoon Rosemary
1 Cup Cream cheese
Black pepper
Water

**Directions**
1. Chop celeriac and cauliflower and add to slow cooker with herbs.
2. Set on low and cook for 2 hours until vegetables are softened.
3. Add cream cheese and ghee and use a masher to blend together. Add pepper and salt to taste and keep warm for 10 minutes.
4. Serve.

**Nutrition Facts (per serving)**
Calories 225
Carbs 7.3g
Protein 5.6g
Fats 20.8g

# Beef Bourguignon

**Ingredients:**
2 lbs. Beef braising steaks
3 Garlic cloves, smashed
750 ml Red wine, dry
4 Cups Mushrooms, white, sliced
1 Teaspoon Salt
3 Tablespoons Lard
1 Onion, chopped
1 Tablespoon Tomato paste, sugar free
8 Bacon slices, chopped
1 Cup Broth
*For Bouquet Garni:*
1 Thyme sprig
3 Cloves
1 Parsley sprig
3 Bay leaves
1 Teaspoon peppercorns

**Directions**
1. Cut up beef and season with pepper and salt.
2. Heat ghee in a skillet and add beef to pot. Cook for 5 minutes until beef is browned. Remove from skillet and transfer to slow cooker
3. Add garlic and onion to skillet and sauté for 2 minutes then transfer to slow cooker.
4. Add broth, wine and tomato paste to cooker and stir together. Place ingredients for garni in a cheesecloth, tie and place into liquid.
5. Set cooker on low and cook for 3 hours until meat is tender.
6. Remove garni and add mushrooms and bacon. Cook for an additional 15 minutes or until mushrooms have softened.
7. Serve. May be served with Cauli-mash.

**Nutrition Facts (per serving)**
Calories 678
Carbs 6.9g
Protein 36.7g
Fats 45g

# Slow Cooker Salmon Pate

**Ingredients:**
1 Tablespoon Ghee
½ Cup Walnuts
½ Cup cream cheese
2 Garlic cloves
½ Teaspoon Salt
2 Salmon filets
1 Onion, chopped
2 Tablespoons Mayonnaise
2 Tablespoons Heavy Cream
2 Tablespoons Lemon juice, fresh
3 Tablespoons Parsley, chopped
Black pepper

**Directions**
1. Add all ingredients except mayonnaise and walnuts and parsley to slow cooker.
2. Set on low and cook for 1 hour until cream cheese is melted. Stir to combine thoroughly then add mayonnaise and adjust salt to taste.
3. Crush walnuts and add to mixture along with parsley.
4. Chill and serve.

**Nutrition Facts (per serving)**
Calories 160
Carbs 1.4g
Protein 7g
Fats 14.4g

# Potato "Gratin"

**Ingredients:**
2 lbs. Rutabaga
1 Onion, chopped
2 Tablespoons Thyme, chopped
3 Cups Chicken broth
1 Teaspoon Salt
3 Tablespoons Ghee
8 Bacon slices
1 Cup Heavy cream
1 Cup Cheddar cheese, shredded
Black pepper
½ Cup Parmesan cheese, grated
½ Cup Sour cream

**Directions**
1. Melt ghee in a skillet and sauté onions for 2 minutes then add bacon.
2. Slice rutabaga and toss with salt.
3. Place a layer of rutabaga into slow cooker, top with some of bacon-onion mixture and then with cheddar cheese. Repeat layers ending with cheese.
4. Combine broth and cream and gently pour around rutabaga. Set cooker on low and cook for 2 hours.
5. Top with sour cream and Parmesan cheese and cook for an additional 30 minutes. Let 'gratin' sit in cooker for 30 minutes to an hour before serving.
6. Serve.

**Nutrition Facts (per serving)**
Calories 445
Carbs 10.2g
Protein 13.9g
Fats 37.7g

# Nacho Chicken Casserole

**Ingredients:**
1 ½ Teaspoons Chili seasoning
4 Oz. Cream cheese
1 Cup tomatoes and green chiles
¼ Cup Sour cream
1 Jalapeno pepper
1 ¾ lbs. Chicken thighs, skinless and boneless
2 Tablespoons Olive oil
4 Oz. Cheddar cheese
3 Tablespoons Parmesan cheese
1 Pack Cauliflower, frozen
Salt
Black pepper

**Directions**
1. Cut up chicken and season with chili seasoning.
2. Heat oil in a skillet and cook chicken until browned all over.
3. Transfer chicken to slow cooker; add sour cream, ¾ of cheddar cheese and cream cheese and stir together.
4. Add chili and tomato paste, mix together. Combine leftover cheese and cauliflower in a processor and pulse until combined and similar to mashed potatoes. Add pepper and salt to taste.
5. Use cauliflower mixture to top chicken in slow cooker and set cooker on low.
6. Cook for 1 hour then top with jalapeno and cook for an additional 30 minutes.
7. Let casserole sit for 30 minutes before serving. Serve.

**Nutrition Facts (per serving)**
Calories 426
Carbs 4.3g
Protein 30.8g
Fats 32.2g

# Kung Pao Chicken

**Ingredients**:
1 Teaspoon Ginger
¼ Cup Peanuts
2 Spring Onions
2 Chicken thighs, with skin and bone
Salt
Black pepper
½ Bell pepper
4 Chilies, Bird's Eye- seeds removed
*For Sauce:*
2 Teaspoons Rice wine vinegar
1 Tablespoon Ketchup, low sugar
½ Teaspoon Maple extract
1 Tablespoon Soy sauce
2 Tablespoon Garlic- Chili paste
2 Teaspoons Sesame oil
Liquid Stevia- 10 drops

**Directions**
1. Cut up chicken and season with pepper and salt.
2. Heat oil in a skillet and cook chicken until browned all over.
3. Transfer chicken to slow cooker. Combine all ingredients for sauce.
4. Add chili to slow cooker then pour sauce all over chicken.
5. Set cooker on low and cooker for 3 hours then add vegetables and peanuts and cook for an additional 15 minutes with cover off.
6. Serve.

**Nutrition Facts (per serving)**
Calories 362
Carbs 3.2g
Protein 22.3g
Fats 27.4g

# Slow Cooker Herbed Lamb

**Ingredients:**
2 lbs. Lamb leg
2 Tablespoons Mustard, whole grain
4 Thyme sprigs
¾ Teaspoon Rosemary
¼ Cup Olive oil
1 Tablespoon Maple syrup
6 Mint leaves
¾ Teaspoon Garlic
Salt
Black pepper

**Directions**
1. Use knife to make 3 slits across lamb.
2. Place lamb into slow cooker and coat with mustard, salt, pepper, oil and maple syrup.
3. Push rosemary and garlic into slits.
4. Set cooker on low and cook for 7 hours then add mint and thyme and cook for an hour more.
5. Let lamb sit for 10 minutes before slicing.
6. Serve.

**Nutrition Facts (per serving)**
Calories 414
Carbs 0.3g
Protein 26.7g
Fats 35.2g

# Cauliflower Shrimp Curry

**Ingredients:**
5 Cups Spinach
1 Onion
1 Cup Coconut milk, unsweetened
¼ Cup Heavy Cream
2 Tablespoons Curry powder
1 Tablespoon Cumin
1 Teaspoon Chili powder
1 Teaspoon Cayenne
½ Teaspoon Ginger
½ Teaspoon Turmeric
¼ Teaspoon Cardamom
¼ Teaspoon Xanthan gum
24 Oz. Shrimp
4 Cups Chicken broth
½ Head Cauliflower
¼ Cup Butter
3 Tablespoon Olive oil
1 Tablespoon Coconut flour
2 Teaspoons Garlic powder
1 Teaspoon Onion powder
1 Teaspoon Paprika
½ Teaspoon Coriander
½ Teaspoon Pepper
¼ Teaspoon Cinnamon
Salt & Black pepper

**Directions**
1. Combine all spices except flour and gum; slice onions.
2. Heat oil in a skillet and cook onion until softened then add cream, spices and butter. Transfer mixture to slow cooker; add broth and coconut milk, stir together and add cauliflower and shrimp.
3. Set cooker on low and cook for 2 hours then combine gum and flour and add to slow cooker along with spinach. Cook for an additional 15 minutes. Serve.

**Nutrition Facts (per serving)**
Calories 331
Carbs 5.6g
Protein 27.4g
Fats 19.5g

# Slow Cooker London Broil

**Ingredients:**
½ Cup Chicken broth
¼ Cup White wine
1 Tablespoon Dijon mustard
2 Teaspoons Onion powder
2 lbs. London Broil
½ Cup Black Coffee
2 Tablespoons Soy sauce
2 Teaspoons Garlic, diced
2 Tablespoons Ketchup, low sugar

**Directions**
1. Combine 1 tablespoon ketchup, 1 teaspoon garlic, 1 tablespoon soy sauce and ½ tablespoon mustard .
2. Use mixture to coat Broil and add to slow cooker. Use onion powder to coat top of Broil.
3. Add liquids to cooker and set on high. Cook for 6 hours then shred.
4. Serve.

**Nutrition Facts (per serving)**
Calories 409
Carbs 2.6g
Protein 47.3g
Fats 18.3g

# BBQ Pulled Chicken

**Ingredients:**
1/3 Cup Butter
¼ Cup Red wine vinegar
¼ Cup Tomato paste, organic
2 Tablespoons Brown mustard, spicy
1 Tablespoon Soy sauce
1 Teaspoon Cumin
1 Teaspoon Fish sauce
6 Chicken thighs, skinless and boneless
¼ Cup Erythritol
¼ Cup Chicken broth
2 Tablespoons Yellow mustard
1 Tablespoon Liquid smoke
2 Teaspoons Chili powder
1 Teaspoon Cayenne pepper

**Directions**
1. Combine all ingredients except chicken and butter in a bowl.
2. Put chicken into slow cooker and pour sauce all over chicken.
3. Set slow cooker on high and cook for 2 hours.
4. Add butter to chicken and set to low, cook for 7 hours. Use forks to shred meat.
5. Serve.

**Nutrition Facts (per serving)**
Calories 510
Carbs 2.3g
Protein 51.5g
Fats 30g

# Orange Cinnamon Beef

**Ingredients:**
3 Cups Beef broth
1 Onion, chopped
Orange Juice, freshly squeezed
1 Tablespoon Thyme
2 Teaspoons Cinnamon
1 ½ Teaspoons Black pepper
1 Teaspoon Soy sauce
1 Teaspoon Rosemary
2 Bay leaves
2 lbs. Beef
3 Tablespoons Coconut oil
Orange zest
2 Tablespoon Apple cider vinegar
2 ½ Teaspoons Garlic, diced
2 Teaspoons Erythritol
1 Teaspoon Salt
1 Teaspoon Fish sauce
1 Teaspoon Sage

**Directions**
1. Cube beef and season with pepper and salt.
2. Heat oil in a skillet until it starts to smoke then add meat a little at a time and cook until browned. Transfer beef to slow cooker.
3. Sauté vegetables in skillet after removing beef. Add orange juice and use spatula to scrape pan then add remaining ingredients except thyme, sage and rosemary.
4. Pour mixture all over beef and mix together.
5. Set slow cooker on high and cook for 3 hours.
6. Add thyme, sage ad rosemary and cook for 2 more hours. Serve.

**Nutrition Facts (per serving)**
Calories 496
Carbs 4.1g
Protein 42.1g
Fats 32.8g

# Italian Sausage and Pepper Soup

**Ingredients**:
1 ½ lbs. Italian sausage, spicy
2 Bell peppers
½ Onion
2 Cups Beef broth
2 Teaspoons Cumin
1 Teaspoon Italian seasoning
6 Cups Spinach
15 oz. Canned Tomatoes with chiles
2 Teaspoons Chili powder
2 Teaspoons Garlic, diced
½ Teaspoon Salt

**Directions**
1. Break sausage into chunks and heat skillet. Cook sausages until browned then transfer to slow cooker.
2. Add broth, spices, tomatoes and peppers to slow cooker and mix together.
3. Sauté garlic and onion until softened then add to slow cooker along with spinach.
4. Set slow cooker on high and cook for 3 hours. Set on low and cook for 2 more hours.
5. Serve.

**Nutrition Facts (per serving)**
Calories 385
Carbs 6.9g
Protein 24g
Fats 27g

# General Tso's Chicken

**Ingredients:**
7 Chicken breasts
1/3 Cup Almond Flour
2 Tablespoons Olive oil
¾ Cup Pork rinds, crushed
2 Eggs
1 Tablespoon Coconut oil
*For sauce:*
3 Tablespoons Rice wine vinegar
2 Tablespoons Ketchup, low sugar
2 Teaspoons Sesame oil
1 Teaspoon Hoisin sauce
1 Teaspoon Red pepper flakes
½ Teaspoon Ginger, diced
¼ Cup Chicken broth
2 ½ Tablespoons Soy sauce
2 Tablespoons Erythritol
1 Teaspoon Garlic powder
1 Teaspoon Red chili paste
¼ Teaspoon Xanthan gum

**Directions**
1. Beat eggs in a small bowl, grind pork rinds and place in another bowl with flour. Heat coconut and olive oil in skillet. Dip chicken in egg and then in pork rinds mixture and fry until crisp.
2. Transfer chicken to slow cooker and mix together the ingredients for the sauce. Pour sauce over chicken.
3. Set slow cooker on high and cook for 2 hours. Stir occasionally to coat chicken.

**Nutrition Facts (per serving)**
Calories 566
Carbs 4.5g
Protein 59.3g
Fats 37.3g

# Pork Hock

**Ingredients**:
1 lb. Pork hock
1/3 Cup Soy sauce
¼ Cup Splenda
1 Tablespoon Butter
1 Teaspoon Five Spice seasoning
2 Garlic cloves, smashed
¼ Cup Rice wine vinegar
1/3 Cup Shaoxing Wine for cooking
½ Onion
Shitake Mushrooms
1 Teaspoon Oregano

**Directions**
1. Heat butter in a skillet and place hocks into pot. Sear until skin is crisp then transfer to slow cooker.
2. Add onions to skillet and sauté then add to slow cooker.
3. Add all remaining ingredients to slow cooker and mix together.
4. Set slow cooker on high and cook for 2 hours then set on low and cook for an additional 2 hours.
5. Take hock from cooker and remove bone, slice and return to sauce.
6. Serve.

**Nutrition Facts (per serving)**
Calories 520
Carbs 8g
Protein 22g
Fats 29g

# Bean-less Chili Con Carne

**Ingredients:**
1 lb. Italian Sausage, spicy
2 Bell peppers
15 Oz. Tomato sauce
2 Tablespoons Chili powder
1 Tablespoon Garlic, diced
1 Tablespoon Butter
1 Teaspoon Salt
1 lb. Ground beef
1 Onion
2 Tablespoons Curry powder
2 Tablespoons Cumin
1 Tablespoon Coconut oil
1 Teaspoon Onion powder
1 Teaspoon Black pepper

**Directions**
1. Heat butter and oil in a skillet then sauté garlic, onion and peppers.
2. Remove from pot and put aside until needed.
3. Add sausage and beef to pot and cook until browned all over, transfer to slow cooker.
4. Add all remaining ingredients, stir together until thoroughly combined.
5. Set slow cooker on high and cook for 4 hours then set on low.
6. Serve.

**Nutrition Facts (per serving)**
Calories 415
Carbs 6g
Protein 29.2g
Fats 25g

# BBQ Chicken Soup

**Ingredients:**
3 Chicken thighs
2 Tablespoons Olive oil
1 ½ Cups Beef broth
2 Teaspoons Chili seasoning
1 ½ Cups Chicken broth
Salt & Black pepper
*For BBQ Sauce:*
¼ Cup Butter
¼ Cup Tomato Paste
1 Tablespoon Soy Sauce
2 ½ Teaspoons Liquid smoke
1 ½ Teaspoons Garlic powder
1 Teaspoon Chili powder
1 Teaspoon Cumin
¼ Cup Ketchup, low sugar
2 Tablespoons Dijon mustard
1 Tablespoon Hot sauce
1 Teaspoon Worcestershire sauce
1 Teaspoon Onion powder
1 Teaspoon Cumin

**Directions**
1. Heat oil in a skillet and season chicken with chili powder, pepper and salt.
2. Sear chicken on both sides until skin is crisp then transfer to slow cooker. Add broths to slow cooker and set on high for 1 hour.
3. Remove chicken from slow cooker, discard skin and bones and return to pot.
4. Combine sauce ingredients and add to slow cooker. Mix together until combined. Add water if necessary.
5. Set slow cooker on low and cook for 1 hour. Serve.

**Nutrition Facts (per serving)**
Calories 487
Carbs 4.3g
Protein 24.5g
Fats 38.3g

# Buffalo Chicken Soup

**Ingredients:**
1 Teaspoon Onion Powder
½ Teaspoon Celery seed
1/3 Cup Hot sauce
1 Cup Heavy cream
¼ Teaspoon
1 ¼ lbs. Chicken thigh, sliced without bones
1 Teaspoon Garlic powder
¼ Cup Butter
3 Cups Beef broth
2 Oz. Cream cheese
Salt
Black pepper

**Directions**
1. Add all ingredients to slow cooker excluding gum and cream cheese.
2. Set slow cooker on low and cook for 6 hours.
3. Take chicken from pot and shred then add gum and cheese to liquid in slow cooker. Use an immersion blender to mix together.
4. Return chicken to pot and mix together.
5. Serve.

**Nutrition Facts (per serving)**
Calories 523
Carbs 3.4g
Protein 20.8g
Fats 44.2g

# Cauliflower and Roasted Bell Pepper Soup

**Ingredients:**
½ Head Cauliflower
3 Green onions, chopped
½ Cup Heavy cream
1 Teaspoon Garlic powder
1 Teaspoon Paprika, smoked
4 Oz. Goat cheese, crumbled
2 Bell peppers, red
6 Tablespoons Duck fat
3 Cups Chicken broth
1 Teaspoon Thyme
¼ Teaspoon Red chili flakes
Salt
Black pepper

**Directions**
1. Place bell peppers onto a baking sheet and broil for 15minutes until charred. Remove from baking sheet and place in a plastic bag.
2. Remove skin from peppers and place into slow cooker with all remaining ingredients except cauliflower and cheese
3. Set slow cooker on low and cook for 2 hours then set on low and add cauliflower. Cook for an additional 1 hour.
4. Serve topped with cheese.

**Nutrition Facts (per serving)**
Calories 345
Carbs 6.2g
Protein 6.4g
Fats 32g

# Slow Cooker Southwestern Pork

**Ingredients:**
1 lb. Pork shoulder, cooked, sliced
2 Teaspoons Cumin
½ Teaspoon Salt
1 Teaspoon Paprika
¼ Teaspoon Cinnamon
6 Oz. Button Mushrooms
½ Onion
1 Bell pepper, sliced
2 Cups Bone broth
¼ Cup Tomato paste
2 Teaspoons Chili powder
1 Teaspoon Garlic, diced
½ Teaspoon Black pepper
1 Teaspoon Oregano
2 Bay leaves
½ Jalapeno, chopped
2 Cups Chicken broth
Lime juice
½ Cup Black Coffee

**Directions**
1. Heat oil in a skillet and sauté vegetables until fragrant.
2. Cube pork and add to slow cooker along with broths, coffee and mushrooms.
3. Add vegetables and spices and mix together.
4. Set slow cooker on low and cook for 4-6 hours.
5. Serve.

**Nutrition Facts (per serving)**
Calories 386
Carbs 6.4g
Protein 19.9g
Fats 28.9g

# <u>Conclusion</u>

Thank you again for purchasing this Freezer Meals Slow Cooker book!

I hope that these recipes were able to show you that the secret to the healthiest and tastiest meals is using fresh, natural, organic and wholesome ingredients. This is all you need for a healthy freezer meals lifestyle and to reap all the benefits of leading a healthy lifestyle, including sustainable weight loss.

The next step is to clean up your eating habits by ditching all the processed, high-carb, toxic and empty calorie foods, that most of us have come to accept as the norm. Making this change won't be a walk in the park, but by making one change at a time, you will start noticing increased energy, decreased cravings and hunger pangs, a faster metabolism, healthy and younger looking skin, among other benefits.

I hope that this diet book was able to show you how the Freezer Meals Slow Cooker Journey can change your life for the best with these simple and super recipes. This is your secret weapon for fighting weight once and for all.

Don't forget to share these recipes with family and friends

Jade Blake